G. Wilkie

Historical and political reflections on the rise and progress of the American rebellion

G. Wilkie

Historical and political reflections on the rise and progress of the American rebellion

ISBN/EAN: 9783743302815

Manufactured in Europe, USA, Canada, Australia, Japa

Cover: Foto ©Suzi / pixelio.de

Manufactured and distributed by brebook publishing software (www.brebook.com)

G. Wilkie

Historical and political reflections on the rise and progress of the American rebellion

HISTORICAL AND POLITICAL

REFLECTIONS

ON THE

RISE AND PROGRESS

OF THE

AMERICAN REBELLION.

IN WHICH

The Causes of that Rebellion are pointed out, and the Policy and Necessity of offering to the AMERICANS a System of Government founded in the Principles of the British Constitution, are clearly demonstrated.

BY

The AUTHOR of LETTERS to a NOBLEMAN, on the Conduct of the AMERICAN WAR.

LONDON:
Printed for G. WILKIE, No. 71, St. Paul's Church-Yard. MDCCLXXX.

[Price 3 s.]

ADVERTISEMENT.

THE following Pamphlet was written in great Haſte, amidſt a multiplicity of other engagements and avocations. It has been publiſhed from the firſt draught, in a manner uncorrected. As the Author found the *American Queſtion* coming forward in Parliament, he thought it his duty to throw what light he could on ſo important a Subject; and he relies on the candour of the Reader to excuſe the literary defects of ſo haſty a performance.

CONTENTS.

The

CONTENTS.

HISTORICAL AND POLITICAL REFLECTIONS ON THE RISE AND PROGRESS OF THE AMERICAN REBELLION.

THE politic, like the natural body, is liable to diſorders, which often terminate in death. To know the cauſe of the diſeaſe in either ſyſtem, is equally neceſſary to a radical cure. This knowledge unattained, the political or phyſical quack will adminiſter his remedies in vain. He may, and indeed often will, throw his patient into agonies and convulſions, and accelerate its death; or by ineffectual remedies give temporary relief, leaving the diſorder to break out again with more dangerous ſymptoms, but cannot expect to give permanent relief.

The American rebellion is an event which has ſtruck deep into the health of the Britiſh ſtate, enfeebled its powers, and, if it has not already produced, it promiſes fair to bring on convulſions, the conſequences of which are not within the reach of human foreſight. From theſe truths we may venture to conclude, that it will be of ſome importance to thoſe who ſuperintend the welfare of the Britiſh ſociety, to be truly informed of the origin of that rebellion; and to be able to trace its progreſs from the original ſpark up to its preſent flame, which has extended ſo wide as to threaten the empire with diſſolution. It is from this knowledge, that a part of the means may be drawn for its immediate ſuppreſſion; and from this alone can that ſyſtem of future polity be formed, which can effect a permanent union between the two countries, and prevent another rebellion from breaking out hereafter with redoubled force and certain ſucceſs.

There are men of reſpectable abilities, and in high ſtations, who have induſtriouſly promoted an opinion, that this unfortunate "and "portentous event has been produced by the in"justice and oppreſſion of the preſent reign,— "by a plan formed by Adminiſtration for enſlav"ing the Colonies." This has been the uniform language of the malcontents on both ſides of the Atlantic. The Congreſs has aſſumed it in order to juſtify their rebellion; and the oppoſition to Government in Britain has echoed it, ſome of them to conceal their thirſt for the emoluments and dignities of office, the ſole ground of their oppoſition; and others, republican in principle, and co-operating in the rebellion, to cover their as yet latent and immature deſign of deſtroying our preſent happy conſtitution. It has been aſſerted ſo often and ſo confidently,

dently, *in* as well as *out* of Parliament, that the incautious, who ſeldom examine the motives of human conduct, have believed it, when leſs credulity and more enquiry would have unveiled its fallacy.

To prove that this opinion is not founded in truth—that neither the conduct of this or any paſt reign ſince the acceſſion of the preſent Royal Family has produced the rebellion in America, but that it has ſprung from very different cauſes, exiſting ſo early as the beginning of the ſixteenth century, and been nouriſhed and fed by thoſe two fiends, Superſtition and Ambition, the great enemies to religious and civil liberty—is the deſign of this Eſſay. But before I proceed to ſupport this opinion, I ſhall endeavour to ſhew the abſurdity and futility of that which I mean to oppoſe It will diſpel the miſt which has been caſt before the eyes of the miſinformed, and enable the candid to perceive the truth in its due force when laid before them.

In almoſt every ſociety, oppoſition to legal government has been a common event. In almoſt every inſtance which hiſtory affords, it has ariſen from a continued ſeries of extreme injuſtice and oppreſſion in the rulers. Theſe have been the *means*, by which ambitious men, of whom every ſociety has its ſhare, have been enabled to incite the vulgar and ignorant to ſedition, and finally to throw off their allegiance. But the American rebellion in this reſpect ſtands diſtinguiſhed from all others. It can appeal neither to antecedent injuſtice nor oppreſſion for an excuſe. At the time it broke out, the people in the Colonies were more free, unincumbered and happy than any others on earth. A ſummary view of the conduct of the State towards the Colonies, from the dawn of their ſettlements to their preſent maturity, will ſupport theſe facts. It will inconteſtably prove, that they have received every encouragement which conſiſted with their own particular intereſt, and which was not adverſe to the general welfare of the ſociety.

Before, as well as ſince, the acceſſion of his preſent Majeſty, the annals of this kingdom will ſhew that the Colonies have been nouriſhed in their infancy, and ſupported in their more adult age, with all the attention of a moſt affectionate parent. If through their own folly they have, in their infant ſtate, quarrelled with their neighbours, their enemies have been conſidered as the enemies of Britain. If their trade has been injured, or their territory invaded, Britain has not failed to reſent the injury. If by repeated acts of fraud and injuſtice done to their innocent and inoffenſive neighbours, they have incurred their hatred and reſentment, Britain has ſtepped in, and by annual donations repaired the injuries, and effected a reconciliation. If the produce of their ſoil was neceſſary to promote the intereſt or ſafety of the community at large, in which their own was of courſe included, generous bounties, to which they did not contribute, were given, as an encouragement to their induſtry, out of the pockets of their Britiſh fellow-ſubjects. If French ambition and Popiſh ſuperſtition have threatened to *annihilate* their civil

civil and religious liberty, the treaſure and blood of Britons have been devoted to their preſervation.

In the two laſt wars, when the powers of France and Spain threatened the deſtruction of their commerce, and the conqueſt of their country, Great-Britain, regardleſs of the expenditure of millions, and the loſs of many thouſands of her ſubjects, by her fleets and armies ſaved them from ruin, leaving them to contribute what proportion of aids *they pleaſed*, towards ſecuring their own ſafety. And to cloſe the ſcene of ineffable benefits beſtowed on theſe ungrateful people, at the concluſion of the laſt war, Great-Britain, unſuſpicious of their ambitious and treacherous deſigns, and inattentive to her own future ſecurity, gave them, by the retention of Canada, abſolute ſafety againſt every enemy, ſave their own ambition, and republican principles. Such were the benefits beſtowed by the State, before the end of the year 1763, without an alloy of one act of intentional injuſtice or oppreſſion, or a ſingle injury done and complained of, which remained unredreſſed. Surely no candid and rational mind can look for the cauſe of rebellion in a conduct ſo truly benevolent.

It is needleſs to ſay more in vindication of the conduct of the State antecedent to the time I have mentioned. The Congreſs themſelves confeſs, that the Colonies have no grievances to complain of before that period. They declare, "that if Government will place them in the "ſituation they were in before the year 1763, "their complaints will ſubſide." Nothing therefore

fore can remain, but to examine whether any acts of injustice or oppression have been done by the State since that time, that could give rise to so open and avowed a rebellion.

The conduct of Government subsequent to this period being grounded on the antecedent circumstances of the Colonies, we must, in this enquiry, look back to the commencement of the last war. At that time France meditated the conquest of British America. Hostilities were begun on the Ohio, within the boundaries of Virginia and Pennsylvania, while vigorous preparations were making to invade New England from Canada. Alarmed at the impending danger, and conscious of their own inability to withstand the power of France, the Colonies supplicated the protection of the Mother-country. A British fleet under Commodore Keppel, and a British army commanded by General Braddock, hastened to their assistance. The strongest of all motives now pressed them to exert their utmost abilities, in defence of their civil and religious rights. No one could suspect that, like the Waggoner in the fable, they would content themselves with supplications only, without putting their shoulders to the wheel. Had a sentiment of that nature prevailed in the British senate, they would certainly have passed laws to compel *them*, on so great an emergency, to a discharge of the first and most important of all political duties. And had this been done, there can be no doubt they would have submitted to, and cheerfully acknowledged, the justice and policy of the measure.

But before the year 1763, America had been considered as in an infant state, capable of contributing little towards the national defence. Just information respecting the amount of her wealth, was wanting. The State, therefore, lest it might unwittingly impose burthens she was not able to sustain, forbore to levy money on her; but confiding in her justice to herself when her own existence was in danger, proceeded by requisitions from the Crown for that purpose; and as an encouragement to a faithful discharge of her duty, Parliament annually engaged to reimburse such of the Colonies as should be liberal in their aids. How far they complied with their reasonable duty, and what their own safety demanded, will be shewn hereafter.

Immediately subsequent to the peace, Great Britain having expended many millions in the defence of the Colonies, the state of America became an object of public investigation. Gentlemen of abilities, who had been sent over for her protection, and had enquired into her circumstances, returned to Britain. From their knowledge, just information poured in upon the great councils of the nation. America was found to contain 2,500,000 people, more than one-fourth of the number in Great Britain. Before the war, the increase of her wealth had been slowly progressive, but during its continuance, rapid and immense. Incredible sums raised on the subjects in this country, and transmitted for the supplies of the navy and army, contributed not a little to her opulence. Her soil produced, in great abundance, every neceſſary to ſupply her own wants, beſides an immenſe ſurplus for exportation. Her freighted ſhips traverſed the ocean to almoſt every port where Britiſh ſubjects were admitted to traffic. The balance of her trade being greatly in her favour, they returned loaded with treaſure, and every luxury which Europe afforded. Their diſſipation was ſcarcely paralleled in Great Britain; and greatly exceeded that ſcanty proportion of aids ſhe had granted upon the requiſition of the Crown.

It further appeared from experience, that the mode of obtaining the colonial aids did not anſwer the purpoſe; for that, numerous and opulent as the people of America were, ſhe had failed of her duty; that the ſums annually granted were, upon the whole, far ſhort of her reaſonable proportion; that ſome of the Colonies gave at one time liberally, at another time nothing; that ſome did not contribute at all towards the burthen of the war, though America was the great object in conteſt; and that this omiſſion of duty aroſe from ſeveral cauſes. The Colonies, in reſpect to each other, were ſo many diſtinct and independent ſocieties, having no political connection among themſelves, nor any authority over each other, by which they could procure the knowledge of each other's circumſtances, neceſſary to aſcertain their reſpective proportions. Nor had they any power to compel them to act in concert for their common ſafety, ſave the ſupreme authority of Great Britain, which had been waved on this occaſion by the mode of ſeparate requiſitions. Thus left to themſelves, they were led and governed by by their diſtinct and ſeparate paſſions, prejudices, and intereſts. Hence thoſe who were moſt expoſed to the immediate aſſaults of the enemy, or were actually invaded, gave liberally, while thoſe that were more diſtant, or were covered by another colony, gave nothing. And even thoſe who had been in the moſt imminent danger, and had received the aſſiſtance of the other Colonies, as ſoon as the danger was removed, refuſed, though called upon, to contribute. The natural conſequence of all which was, that the ſums granted by Great Britain in the beginning of the war were waſted; the expeditions, concerted for their own ſafety, failed; the Britiſh troops were defeated, and the lives of many thouſands of their Britiſh fellow-ſubjects, ſent over for their protection, by their parſimony and injuſtice were ſacrificed; the war was protracted; and the State was obliged to impoſe immenſe additional taxes on its ſubjects in Britain, to ſupply the deficiencies ariſing from the refractory conduct and ingratitude of thoſe in America.

Such was the ſtate and conduct of America during the laſt war; and ſuch it muſt have continued ſo long as the Crown ſhould rely on drawing from the Colonies a reaſonable proportion of aids, by the mode of requiſitions. At the concluſion of that war, a Miniſter was at the helm, to whoſe abilities, firmneſs of mind, and love of public juſtice, future hiſtorians, when the influence of prejudice and party ſhall ceaſe, will pay the juſt tribute. This Miniſter perceiving the involuntary inability in the Colonies, ariſing from their diſunited ſtate, and the voluntary injustice arising from their passions, prejudices, and separate interests; and viewing in its full force the absurdity of expecting an equitable proportion of aids towards the national defence from them, when not only the quantity, but the contribution itself, was left at their pleasure, resolved to drop the ill-advised and ineffectual mode of requisition.

But he could not stop here. He held a trust, from which every subject had a right to expect an equal distribution of the burthens of society. Was he to continue those burthens on three-fourths of the subjects of the empire, and to permit the other fourth to be exempted? Was he to suffer the opulence of America to increase, and her sons to riot in luxury and dissipation, without contributing a reasonable proportion of those aids which were necessary to her own safety? Was he to commit yet greater injustice to his country, by insuring that safety, in future, by those aids which were to be raised on the people in Great Britain alone, already labouring under an immense debt incurred by the American war? Public justice, and the most sacred of all temporal obligations, his public duty, forbad it.

What other method then could he pursue, save that which was founded in a multitude of precedents, and which the constitution of the British government directed? The exercise of supreme authority by the State over the Colonies was that method; he knew, that the injudicious mode of requisitions had been adopted on account of the want of information. That information was now obtained. He knew, that

a perfect

a perfect ſubordination of the Coloniſts had been eſtabliſhed, by the patents and proclamations under which they were originally ſettled—that their right to the territory had been granted by the repreſentative and truſtee of the Britiſh Society, under its great ſeal, reſerving rents in lieu of ſervices—that the oaths of allegiance had ever been taken by the Coloniſts to him as that repreſentative—that all their civil and political rights had been derived from, and were held under, him in that capacity—that the common law of the realm, and the ſtatutes made before their ſettlement, had been extended—that innumerable laws for regulating their trade, reſtraining their manufactures, directing their internal police, and levying taxes both internal and external, were to be found in the volumes of Britiſh ſtatutes—and that every document of the State, relative to America, were ſo many demonſtrations, and almoſt every act of the Colonies, reſpecting Great Britain, were ſo many inconteſtible recognitions, of their ſubordination to the ſupreme authority of the Britiſh empire, in all caſes whatſoever.

In this light, the light in which all antecedent Miniſters, all preceding Parliaments, and the Coloniſts themſelves, had on all occaſions conſidered America, the Miniſter conſidered it. The national defence being the firſt great object of his duty, and an equal diſtribution of the burthens neceſſary for that purpoſe the next in importance—he propoſed the Stamp Act in parliament, in their ſeſſion 1763, which paſſed into a reſolve. Of this reſolution the Colonies had official notice. They were told, " unleſs they would

" grant a juſt and reaſonable proportion of aids " in their ſeveral Aſſemblies, or ſhould point out " ſome mode by which it might be done more " agreeably to themſelves, national juſtice re- " quired, that the act ſhould paſs in the next " ſeſſion." The reſolve of the Houſe of Commons, and the notice from the Miniſter, were conſidered by the American Aſſemblies. A year elapſed, and no aids were granted, no other mode was hinted to Parliament, and no objection was made either to the equity or burthen of the tax, or to the mode of raiſing it, or to the authority by which it was to be levied, except only by the Maſſachuſſett's and Virginia Aſſemblies, who reſted in a denial of the conſtitutional authority of Parliament, without granting, or offering to grant, their reaſonable proportion of aids to the national defence. The act therefore paſſed unanimouſly. Indeed, no law within the compaſs of human wiſdom could be found more juſt and adequate to its purpoſe;—none better calculated to diſcover the juſt proportions of the wealth poſſeſſed by the ſeveral Colonies;—none better to eſtabliſh a juſt diſtribution of the tax among them;—nor any which could ſo effectually carry its own powers into execution.

The fate of this ſtatute, equally unfortunate to both countries, is univerſally known. Its execution was oppoſed by a ſmall intereſted faction in America, and that faction was vindicated and ſupported in Britain. It was repealed on principles void of reaſon or juſtice, and contrary to the moſt evident policy. The perſeverance and firmneſs of the Miniſter ſtood oppoſed by the timidity and groundleſs fears of the C—b—t.

The

The latter prevailed; and the Minister foreseeing the measure portentous of events equally important and mischievous to the welfare of the society, reluctantly deserted the service of his country, which he had in vain attempted to promote.

A foresight of the mischiefs which would flow from the repeal of this statute, was not confined to the Minister who proposed it. They were *seen* by many in the great councils of the State, they were feared by some in the C—b—t, and they were even within the shallow comprehension of the Minister who succeeded him, and by whose factious influence the repeal had been effected. Even this Minister dreaded the consequences of his own conduct. He knew, that the remonstrances of the Colonies rested in a denial of the supreme authority of the State. He foresaw, that the repeal of the act, *on that ground*, would naturally lead to a like denial in respect to every other matter cognisable in Parliament. He could not suspect, that those who had presumed to deny its power in a matter the most important to its existence, the most momentous to the safety of society, and more particularly to their own, would hesitate to oppose it in others of infinitely less moment. He knew, and he believed that others knew, that he had been surrendering up to groundless clamours, in which the sinister views of his own ambition had united, the most important right of the supreme authority of the State, a right to command the aids necessary to the national defence; that he had destroyed that unity of power in the British, which has ever been found

essential

essential in the constitution of all states, and without which the members of no society can be compelled to act in concert for the general safety; and of course, that he had laid a broad foundation for the independence of America.

Alarmed at the prospect of these mischiefs, shame and regret took place for a moment of his ambition. He endeavoured to heal the wound, which the dagger from his own hand had made in the British empire. The remedy applied was the Declaratory Act. In order to make this palatable to his factious American friends, he *treacherously* undertook to assure them, without any authority from Parliament, "that though the act was declaratory of the "right, yet Government never would attempt "to exercise it." The Colonies were to be considered in the most absurd of all lights; as members of the British society, and yet independent of its sovereign authority;—as so many distinct inferior politic bodies, without any political subordination;—as so many little *imperia in imperio*;—as members possessed of the most perfect justice and integrity;—as devoid of human prejudices, attachments or frailties, and left to their own pleasure to do what justice they should think proper to a people who had saved them from ruin, and were bound to protect them in future.

No man, acquainted with those motives which ever yet have produced a revolt in society, can believe, that either of the before-mentioned acts could be the original cause of the rebellion. The principle of the first was confessed to be just, and the burthen imposed was ſo light as not to be made an object of complaint; and the ſecond neither did or could do them an injury. It neither impoſed a burthen, nor deprived the Colonies of a right. It was only declaratory of that authority, to which they had ſubmitted from the firſt dawn of their ſettlement. Indeed, the enacting and repeal of the Stamp Act, and the paſſing of the Declaratory Bill, with the mean and contemptible aſſurances attending it, diſcovered ſuch a want of firmneſs and ſtability in the Britiſh councils, as to afford juſt matter for American ridicule, not reaſon for complaint, much leſs for ſedition and rebellion. That theſe tranſactions had their effects, muſt be confeſſed; for though they cannot be ſaid to have been the original cauſe of the rebellion, yet it is known to every obſervant American, that ſo much timidity and weakneſs in the councils of this country tended to encourage and nouriſh the ſeeds of American ſedition, long before planted, and now growing faſt to a dangerous maturity.

The numbers of people, the commerce and opulence of America, ſtill increaſing with amazing rapidity; the trifling debt incurred by the laſt war being nearly paid off, and Great Britain labouring under an enormous debt, a great part of which was incurred in meaſures for her protection; repeated demands having been made, by the Crown, of the Aſſemblies, to grant the neceſſary ſums for the ſupport of the adminiſtration of their own juſtice, to no purpoſe; and the deficiency being conſtantly ſupplied by monies raiſed on the people of Great Britain,

tain, already overburdened with debt; were ſo many circumſtances which ſtared every Miniſter in the face as he came into office. To be altogether inattentive to theſe conſiderations, was more than an honeſt mind, intruſted with the adminiſtration of national juſtice, could ſupport. Beſides, as matters then ſtood upon the American remonſtrances againſt the Stamp Act, the repeal of that Act, the Declaratory Act, and the ſubſequent aſſurances from the Miniſter, the authority of the Parliament over the Colonies was in a manner given up. It was therefore neceſſary, not only in point of juſtice, but policy, to paſs the Act commonly called the Tea Act.

This act has alſo been enumerated in the liſt of American grievances, and as one of the cauſes of the preſent rebellion. Let us enquire into the fact. So much of the regulations of this act as related to the impoſition of duties on foreign paper, glaſs, and painters' colours, was indeed unjuſt. Of this, complaint was made; and the juſtice of the Britiſh Parliament immediately interpoſed, becauſe it ſubjected the people of America to a double duty, one payable in Britain, another in America. But the duty on tea remained unrepealed, becauſe no ſuch objection lay to it. The Parliament had, in framing the act, taken off the foreign duty of one ſhilling payable in Great Britain, and laid only threepence on the pound payable in America. Now, if the duties on the other articles were an unjuſt burden on the ſubject in America, it was immediately relieved, and the one impoſed on teas was an abundant favour.

It

It enabled them to import that article ninepence in the pound cheaper than they could import it before paſſing the act.

Of the juſtice done to the Colonies in the repeal of the duties on paper, glaſs, and painters' colours, and of the favour done in enabling them to drink their tea, which made ſo great a part of their ſubſiſtence, ninepence in the pound cheaper than they had ever purchaſed before, the Americans were truly ſenſible. In vain did the Republicans of New-England ſet every engine at work, and exert their endeavours, by their partizans in every Colony, to prevail on the merchant not to import, and the people not to buy the article of tea. In vain did they enter into a non-importation agreement. The merchant would, and did import, and the people, led by their true intereſt, would, and did buy, notwithſtanding all their exertions to prevent it.

In order to do a further favour to the people of America, to the prejudice of the Britiſh American merchant, but to the benefit of the Eaſt India Company, an act was paſſed to enable the Company, by their agents, to ſell their teas in America by lots, in the ſame manner they were ſold in Great Britain. I call this a favour to the people of America. By this act, the ſhopkeeper or retailer, in the ſea-port towns, was enabled to purchaſe his tea in lots, incumbered only with the freight from Great Britain to America. The conſumer of tea in America was obliged to pay only one profit to the Company, another to the ſhopkeeper. But before the act, they uſually paid a profit to the Company, to the London merchant who bought it of the Company, and ſold it to the American merchant, and alſo to the American merchant, beſides the profit of the retailer. So that, by this act, the conſumer of this neceſſary and common article of ſubſiſtence was enabled to purchaſe it at one half of its uſual price; an advantage that did not, nor could eſcape the moſt vulgar comprehenſion.

The next act enumerated in the liſt of American grievances, is that prohibiting the trade of Boſton, until the corporation ſhould pay the damages wantonly done to the Eaſt India Company. Had the Parliament proceeded further, and deprived the corporation of every privilege it contained on the ſame terms, no juſt man would have called it ſevere: Becauſe, however weighty might have been the burthen, their relief from it was left in their own power, and the condition of relief was nothing more than a ſtrict act of juſtice, which reſted with them to perform or not, at their pleaſure. This was the opinion of all America, ſave a few men who meant to make uſe of it as an inſtrument to deceive and miſlead the ignorant and incautious into rebellion. Even the inhabitants of the Maſſachuſſett's province, when called upon to unite in oppoſition to this act, told the Select Men of Boſton, That their corporation had done an act of violence and injuſtice, by deſtroying the property of their fellow-ſubjects, and that they only ought to make reparation, and by it relieve themſelves from the diſtreſs brought on them by their own unjuſt conduct.

The laſt in the liſt is, the act for altering one article in the Maſſachuſſett's charter, which takes from the General Court, or Aſſembly, the right of conſtituting the middle branch of the legiſlature, and veſts it ſolely in the King's repreſentative. I ſhall not now enter on a detail of the miſchiefs to the peace and welfare of the province, which had ariſen from the want of this regulation. They are notorious to every one acquainted with its political hiſtory, and they are briefly recited in the ſubſequent part of theſe remarks. It is enough to ſay, they were intolerable, and had been found by long experience to be totally inconſiſtent with its ſubordination to the Britiſh empire.

When our preſent happy conſtitution was ſettled, it was the intention of our anceſtors that it ſhould be permanent and unalterable. It was wiſely formed, equally to avoid the oppreſſion and miſchiefs ariſing from abſolute monarchy and democracy, from tyranny and licentiouſneſs. The authority of the Crown, and the privileges of the people, were ſo placed in oppoſite ſcales, as always, when rightly informed, and acting on principles which lead to their mutual ſafety, to be on an equal balance. But as the monarch and the people were both ſubject to human frailties, and naturally fond of unlimited power, an independent ariſtocratical authority was ſo appointed, as to be able to throw its weight in either ſcale, as the other ſhould preponderate. By this policy alone the duration and freedom of the Britiſh government has been maintained for ages paſt, and may be maintained for ages to come, if ſtrictly adhered to. How often this ariſtocratical power has been thrown into the different ſcales, and how much oftener into the popular than the monarchical, to preſerve the conſtitution, may be ſeen in our hiſtory. Now the right of appointing this ariſtocratical part of the Britiſh government, has been fixed and eſtabliſhed in the Crown from the firſt dawn of the preſent government. The people of England have never claimed, nor pretended to claim it; and I am ſure, that no King was ever authoriſed to give away any of the rights of the Crown. They are fiduciary truſts, unalienably veſted in him and his ſucceſſors for ever, for the benefit of the ſociety. They were conferred on him, to maintain the rights of Government, and not to deſtroy them. But by this grant of the ariſtocratical rights of the conſtitution to a part of the commonalty of the empire, the King aſſumed a power by which he might, at his pleaſure, deſtroy the eſſence of the Britiſh government, ſubvert its balance, and throw it into inextricable confuſion. For, if he may grant them to the ſubjects of the State emigrating to America, he may certainly grant them to thoſe who remain in Britain. The moſt artful reaſoner cannot contradict this truth without apparent ſophiſtry; becauſe no reaſon can be aſſigned why he may grant to the ſubjects of the State ſettling out of the realm, rights which he cannot grant to thoſe within it; and if, by the fundamental laws of the State, he holds a right to grant theſe powers to the people of Britain, he may, at his pleaſure, deſtroy the conſtitution of the Britiſh government.

Supported

Supported by theſe principles, I may ſurely affirm, that no King of England was ever veſted with a right to grant to the people of the Maſſachuſſett's legiſlature, the ſole appointment, or a ſhare in the appointment, of the ariſtocratic part of its conſtitution; that Parliament poſſeſſed authority to alter the charter of Boſton in this particular, and in every other where the powers granted were inconſiſtent with fundamental laws and the eſtabliſhed conſtitution of the ſtate; and not only the charter of Maſſachuſſett's, but every other charter granted to the Colonies, whoſe powers tend to weaken either the monarchical, ariſtocratical, or democratical balance of the Britiſh Government; and that it was their duty indiſpenſible to make ſuch alteration; and not only to do this, but to proceed in the work till every Colony charter is made conformable to the true fundamental principles of a mixed monarchy; becauſe theſe alterations are not only evidently neceſſary to the ſafety of the ſtate, but alſo to the happineſs of the Coloniſts themſelves.

But it has been ſaid, that this act gave the univerſal alarm throughout America. This is an aſſertion without any foundation in reaſon or truth. It could alarm none but thoſe who were already attached to democratical principles, and in whoſe breaſts an averſion to the Britiſh Government was already fixed. All the loyaliſts throughout the Colonies rather approved of than condemned the meaſure. It affected no Colony but the Maſſachuſſett's immediately, and none in proſpect, ſave Connecticut and Rhode-Iſland; and even in theſe, the men whoſe intereſt

intereſt and honours did not depend on popular aſſemblies and popular confuſion, thought it juſt and neceſſary. In Pennſylvania the people had petitioned for a Royal Government, in which this meaſure was included and approved; and in Maryland, and all the Royal Governments, it had been eſtabliſhed from the firſt ſettlement of their Colonies. The Pennſylvanians could not, therefore, be alarmed at a meaſure which conferred on their fellow-coloniſts the very boon they had prayed for themſelves: nor could the people of Maryland, and the Royal Governments, be ſuppoſed to reſent, or be diſguſted at this act of the State, inaſmuch as this right had been exerciſed by the governors of their own provinces without the leaſt murmur or complaint, ever ſince their ſettlement.

When theſe acts, which are the great ſubjects of American complaints, are impartially conſidered, what do we find in them to ſupport thoſe complaints? What, that has the leaſt appearance of a deſign in Government to enſlave the Colonies? The reader has now before him the principles upon which theſe ſtatutes were made. He perceives that the Stamp Act was paſſed to draw a reaſonable revenue from Colonies which had been, and muſt continue to be, protected by the State—That the Declaratory Act was rendered neceſſary by the conduct of the Colonies, to ſupport the ſupremacy of Parliament, which they had denied—That the Tea Act was deſigned to procure a revenue from them, but in a manner ſo beneficial, that for every three pence paid they received one ſhilling. The act for altering the Maſſachuſſett's charter only declared that to be void which was void in itſelf, becauſe granted without authority, and annulled an unconſtitutional power, which was really miſchievous to the people themſelves. The Boſton Port Act was no more than an act of common and natural juſtice. What was it the duty of Adminiſtration to have done? Were they to ſuffer the burthen of American protection to lie longer heavy on the ſhoulders of the people of this country? Were Britons to become *hewers of wood, and drawers of water*, for an American faction? Were they tamely to permit the ſupreme authority of the State to be inſolently trampled on by its ungrateful ſubjects, without ſupporting it? Were they to hear the calls for juſtice from Britiſh ſubjects, againſt the acts of violence of the Boſton faction, and not give them redreſs? And were ſtatutes made for thoſe purpoſes, ſupported as they are by the principles of all laws human and divine, to be tortured by any ſophiſtry into cauſes ſufficient to juſtify rebellion? If there is a man living, who will ſubſcribe to the affirmative of theſe queſtions, with him I will not contend.

Having thus ſhewn that the American rebellion has not ariſen from thoſe motives to which the rebels in America, and their adherents in Britain, have artfully and falſely imputed them, with intent to conceal their own flagitious deſigns, we will ſearch for Truth where ſhe is only to be found; and endeavour to demonſtrate by what *progreſſive* means, and fatal ſucceſſion of events, the original ſpark has been produced, and nouriſhed up to its preſent flame; which by

its

its extenſive influence has deſtroyed the peace of Great-Britain, and ſeems to endanger its exiſtence as an independent empire.

To do this, we muſt look as far back into the political hiſtory of this country, as the beginning of the ſixteenth century. At this period, Chriſtianity in Britain was delivered from the ſhackles of the church of Rome. Henry VIII. Edw. VI. and Queen Elizabeth had performed the generous taſk. Under their auſpices the church of England became eſtabliſhed; but too *rigidly* attached to her own doctrines and modes of worſhip, her rules admitted of little latitude or indulgence for different opinions. That reſtraint on the conſciences of men, from which ſhe had ſo lately been relieved, was, by herſelf, too ſtrictly impoſed on others. That freedom of the human mind, which is not always to be reſtrained by the wiſeſt regulations, and which was rather increaſed than diminiſhed by the Reformation, remained yet too much limited. The zeal, I may call it rage, for more liberty in religion, ſoon broke the bounds of that reſtraint, and multiplied into a variety of ſects diſſenting from the Church. Theſe ſhe haraſſed and diſtreſſed. Among the perſecuted were the Puritans, or *Firſt Independents*; and none felt the weight of her power with more ſeverity.

At this conduct in the Church we ſhall not be ſurpriſed, when we review the principles of theſe ſectaries; their religious tenets were altogether heterodox, and their principles of eccleſiaſtical polity were as directly repugnant to thoſe of the eſtabliſhed Church, as their ideas of civil government were to thoſe of a mixed monarchy;

narchy; and of course equally inconsistent with the safety of both.

By the 25th of Henry VIII. the King had been declared the supreme head of the church. From him flowed all ecclesiastical promotions; by him the bishops were appointed; under him all the inferior clergy held their offices; and the rules of the church were established by his authority: but these sectaries held it a maxim too sacred to be dispensed with, that the power of their church could be subject to no temporal authority whatsoever; that it was a separate independent body, governed by the ordinances of their king Jesus, which they expounded according to their own fanatic and excentric notions; that the privilege and power of electing and ordaining ministers of the gospel was, of right, vested in the people; that they who held the right to invest with, must hold the right to dispossess a minister of, his power and office; and that all offences against good morals and the rules of their church, ought to be heard and determined by the people, or congregational communicants, from whose decision there could be no lawful appeal to any temporal authority whatever.

It was not to be expected that people possessed of these notions, and who had adopted them as sacred tenets of conscience, could ever make good and faithful subjects to a state, where the licentiousness of popular power was checked and restrained by that of monarchy and aristocracy. This kind of popular independence in ecclesiastical, was so nearly allied to that in civil polity, it is scarcely possible to conceive that the human mind could hold the one and reject the other. That kind of reason which led to the one, as strongly inculcated the other; and the principle of either was the principle of both. They therefore maintained, that the right to all *civil* as well as *ecclesiastical* power originated in the people, and ought to remain vested in them without any controul. If these doctrines, so manifestly inconsistent with the principles of the British constitution, taught the Puritans to believe that an independent popular Government in their own hands could alone effectually secure their independence in religion, it at the same time convinced the established Government and Church, that their safety (in the then infant state of the Reformation, which required an union in sentiment to support it) depended on suppressing them.

Zealously attached to their own notions, a number of these sectaries, to avoid the persecution in Britain, emigrated to Holland, in hopes of finding a Government more favourable to their designs. Here they were received with every indulgence the freedom of the human mind could desire. They erected churches, settled congregations, established among themselves their own church-government, and lived without molestation. But this did not satisfy them; they were not happy. One and the first object of their enthusiasm, the possession of a government of their own purely republican, was not gratified, nor likely to be so under the States. An aristocratic society was as different from their ideas of civil polity, as a mixed monarchy. They, therefore, resolved to go in ſearch of further adventures in another country. The Hollanders laboured to perſuade them to ſettle under their ſtates with their people on Hudſon's river : but this did not anſwer their purpoſe. They choſe to be in a country alone, unmixed with others, and to have all power in their own poſſeſſion. That country was New-England ; and neither the dangers of an ocean rarely explored, nor of a wilderneſs filled with ſavages, could divert them from their purpoſe.

In the year 1620 they arrived, and ſettled *New Plymouth.* Here they ſet up their own modes of worſhip and form of government. And as the two great objects of their emigration were an independent church, and a republican ſociety, they inſtituted both ; veſting the powers of direction and puniſhment, in all caſes whatſoever, in the people at large. All their officers were elective ; and when elected, they exerciſed all the powers of government, legiſlative, executive, and fœderative ; but under forms and ceremonies as different as poſſible from thoſe of the ſtate whoſe territory they poſſeſſed, and whoſe ſubjects they were : and all this was done without the leaſt authority from the Britiſh Government. In this manner they lived until the year 1629, when they obtained a grant for their territories from the Council of Plymouth, which I ſhall have occaſion ſoon more particularly to mention.

The beginning of the reign of Charles I. was not more remarkable for toleration, than that of his immediate predeceſſor. A perſecution of the Nonconformiſts continued. The

Puritans, among others, were *harassed* and *suffered.* Their principles of religion and polity were in no essential different from those of the Brownists or Independents; and their spirits and enthusiasm were equally intolerant of the rules of the established church and government. The path to America being now explored by their brethren the Brownists, whose settlement had considerably increased, a number of these sectaries also resolved to settle in New England. To countenance their design, they purchased of the Plymouth Company a part of their territory. But it contained no powers to institute civil policy. To what reason this omission was owing, is not positively known. It could not be occasioned by a reluctance in the grantees to accept of them, because they were necessary to their safety, and the accomplishment of their views. It is therefore more than probable, when we consider that the grantors were Lords of his Majesty's Council, and other noblemen and gentlemen, all of them members of the established church, that they would not entrust men of such dangerous principles to the church and state, with the powers of government in a distant country. However, this omission obliged them to apply to the Crown for a charter, which they obtained March 4, 1628.

Upon a view of this charter, sundry observations occur too important to be omitted. Nine tenths of the grantees were Nonconformists, composed of a mixture of Puritans and Presbyterians. The powers and privileges asked for and granted were merely republican. Every

prero-

prerogative of the Crown, and all the rights of the ariſtocratic part of the Britiſh conſtitution, were ſacrificed to the republican views of the grantees.

By this charter the grantees were conſtituted a body politic, with all the rights neceſſary to form a complete independent civil ſociety. They were veſted with a power to receive into and make free of their ſociety ſuch perſons as "they ſhould think fit;" to chuſe annually their own Governor, Deputy-Governor, and aſſiſtants out of the perſons ſo denizen'd; and in theſe were veſted as full and complete a legiſlative power, as that of the King, Lords, and Commons, ſo far as regarded the territory granted and the inhabitants of it. Or, in the words of the charter, they were impowered "to make laws "and ordinances for the good and welfare of "the Company, and for the government of "the lands and plantations, and the people "inhabiting and to inhabit the ſame, as to them, "from time to time, ſhould be thought meet."

There was no other controul to this complete legiſlative authority, than that the laws and ordinances ſhould not be contrary or repugnant to the laws and ſtatutes of the realm. And, in reſpect to this, there was not the leaſt proviſion that theſe legiſlators ſhould tranſmit their acts for the repeal or even inſpection of the State, nor any authority reſerved in the Crown to demand ſuch tranſmiſſion; nor in caſe of refuſal, a forfeiture or penalty to enforce it. So that even this controul was inſignificant.

Nor was this charter leſs liberal in granting away the executive rights and prerogatives of the

the Crown. The grantees held under it full powers to settle the "forms and ceremonies of "government and magistracy," and to "name "and style all sorts of officers, both superior "and inferior, distinguishing and setting forth "the several duties, powers, and limits of "every such office," and the "forms of the "oaths to be respectively ministered unto them;" "to dispose and order the election of all such "officers;" and to impose all "fines, imprison-"ments, and other lawful corrections" on the people. To which was added the right of making war and peace, under no other restrictions than those contained in the laws of nature and nations. Thus all the powers of the State, legislative, executive, and even fœderative were given up by their charter. An *imperium in imperio*, or a government which was intended to be dependent and subordinate, was established with independent powers. But more; the charter is so far from confining the essential principles of their polity to those of the parent state, that every power, right, and privilege granted, is purely democratical. All of them originate with, and once in every year revert to popular assemblies, without a single ray of monarchy or aristocracy mixed with them.

A charter thus framed exactly accorded with the Puritanic and democratical wishes and principles of the grantees, and the people who were to be governed by it. But by what means the powers of government and dominion, so totally inconsistent with the supreme legislative authority of the state, so subversive of the rights of of the Crown, and in all respects repugnant to the established form of a mixed monarchy, could be obtained from a King, whose evident design was to extend his prerogatives beyond their constitutional bounds, is at this day difficult to ascertain. The most probable conjecture is, that they were obtained by corruption. Indeed this opinion seems founded in something more than conjecture. Documents of some credit say, that the large sum of two thousand pounds was paid for the purchase. This will appear yet more probable, when we consider the perplexity and distress which the Court of Charles was often subjected to for want of money. Indeed it seems impossible to account for it otherwise; for it exceeds all the bounds of reasonable conjecture, that a Prince, possessed of such high ideas of the extent of his prerogative, should grant a charter effectually subversive of that prerogative, on any other ground than that of necessity.

However this may be, it was not reasonable to expect that men, governed by these principles, and possessed of the unlimited powers of this charter, would ever adopt the laws of England, or even found their own laws upon the same principles; much less that they would retain an attachment to, or even a favourable opinion of, the principles of the English Government. All experience in the political history of man—the influence which different civil polity ever had, and will have, on the human passions and affections, forbad it. If we would remove vicious habits, manners, or opinions inconsistent with the unity and safety of the society,

prohibitory

prohibitory laws must be made to suppress them. If we would form or maintain salutary habits, manners, or opinions consistent with the interest of a society, preceptive laws must be made to inculcate and support them. These maxims are founded in common sense, in common policy, and in almost universal practice. But this charter, by some strange inattention, influence, or infatuation in the Government that granted it, was manifestly calculated to efface all the laws, habits, manners, and opinions which it ought to support, to destroy that system of polity which it ought to have maintained, and to level all the orders, arrangements, checks, and balances, wisely graduated and tempered, of a mixed monarchy, to the lowest and most imperfect of all political systems, a tumultuous, seditious, and inert democracy. How far this assertion is just, we shall perceive in tracing the conduct of the people who settled under it.

I have mentioned before, that the first settlers in New England had nothing less in view than an independent establishment, both in religion and government. For these reasons they first left England, and emigrated to Holland; they left Holland, and ventured to New England; and they and their friends, united with them in religious and political opinions, obtained the charter now under consideration. It was certainly the intent of the charter, that the corporation should be established in England, and that the colonists under it should be governed by the general laws of the realm, and the particular laws made by the corporation thus established. But the penetration of these enthu-

siasts

ſiaſts ſoon diſcovered, or perhaps it was known to them before, that the powers of an inferior corporation, under the immediate eye and controul of the ſupreme authority of the State, however unlimited their powers from the Crown, would not venture to eſtabliſh their independence, or at leaſt would not be ſo bold in doing it, as one at three thouſand miles diſtance, where their laws, their manners, and conduct might be concealed or diſguiſed from the penetration of the State. It was therefore agreed by the corporation, within eighteen months after it had been eſtabliſhed in England, to remove all its powers to America, without the leaſt authority from the Crown for that purpoſe.

Previous to the charter they had given evident proofs of their deſign. They had eſtabliſhed a form of government altogether popular, and a church on congregational principles. They had aboliſhed the uſe of the common prayer and ſervice of the church of England. An attempt to perform it in a particular ſociety, collected for that purpoſe, was adjudged ſedition againſt the government, and two of the members of their council were baniſhed from the community for that offence.

Upon the removal of their charter, they thought, that the foundation of their independence was laid. By what means they erected the ſuperſtructure is a curious enquiry; it is alſo a neceſſary one to unfold the genuine ſpirit of the people, and to lead us to the cauſes of the preſent rebellion. A Government was ſoon eſtabliſhed, altogether democratical. A Governor, Deputy governor, an Aſſiſtant, and a Magiſtracy were appointed; —and as the firſt great object was the eſtabliſhment of their own religion, to the excluſion of the Church of England, and all other denominations of Chriſtians, the firſt law of any moment that was enacted, declared, "that none ſhould be admitted to the freedom of the body politic, but ſuch as were members of their own church." By this law, made directly contrary to the evident deſign of the charter, which gave any ſubject a right to ſettle in New England, a majority of the people then in that country were deprived of their civil rights and privileges, rendered incapable of holding any place of honour or profit, and liable to be tried for all offences by perſons adverſe in opinions and ſentiments to them. The illegality and cruelty of this act were obvious; it was as repugnant to the dictates of reaſon and humanity, as it was inconſiſtent with the ſpirit and deſign of the charter. And yet it continued in force until the diſſolution of their charter, or upwards of ſixty years. But it was neceſſary to the excluſive eſtabliſhment of their church; and to this meaſure whatever appeared neceſſary, was in the opinion of their Government lawful and juſt.

It was not long before they found, that this law, although it effectually deprived all perſons of different perſuaſions in religion from participating in their Government, it did not prevent their ſettling in the territory. Many, indeed a majority of the ſettlers, differed from them in religious ſentiments and modes of worſhip, and many others were expected from England, with

deſign

defign to purchafe and fettle; all which tended to fubvert their original defign of referving the government and territory of New England to themfelves, "the only chofen people of God." Alarmed at this profpect, an act yet more unjuft, and more repugnant to the fpirit of the charter, was paffed. All perfons were forbid to entertain in their houfes any ftranger, who came with intent to refide among them, without liberty from one of the ftanding council, or two other affiftants. The penalties were as fevere as the law was unjuft. Forty pounds were impofed on every perfon who fhould receive fuch ftranger, and twenty pounds for every month he remained with him, and one hundred pounds on any town which fhould give or fell to him a lot of ground to refide on.

Thus the fame people, who had lately been perfecuted, became the perfecutors. It would be tedious to mention in detail all the cruelties committed under the authority of their fynod, and this democratical government. It would exhibit a picture of human folly and wickednefs more painful than entertaining. I fhall only therefore remark, that all the fubjects of the ftate, who held different opinions of religion, were deemed either libellous againft the church, feditious againft the government, or blafphemous againft their God. Every tenet of religion inconfiftent with their own, was adjudged heterodox and heretical. We cannot therefore be furprifed, upon looking into the hiftory of their government, to find inftances of inquifitorial cruelty. Toleration in the rulers was deemed a fin which would bring down the judgments of heaven upon the land. Inquiſition was made into men's private judgments, as well as their declarations and practice. Many innocent and inoffenſive people were imprisoned, many baniſhed on pain of ſuffering death in caſe they returned, and ſome were condemned and ſuffered death; and all the rights of conſcience and humanity were violated and ſuppreſſed, although, by the words of the charter, toleration in religion and full liberty of conſcience were expreſsly granted. If any reaſonable mind can deſire further evidence than theſe tranſactions, that the people now ſettled in New England intended to exclude all perſons of every other religion but their own, and to ſet up an independent popular republic in that country, it will appear from the declaration of their favourite governor, Mr. Winthrop, who muſt be ſuppoſed to be perfectly acquainted with their views. For he ſays, in a letter wrote to Lord Say, that "God had "choſen New England to plant *his people* in, "and that it would be diſpleaſing to him that "*this work* ſhould be hindered."

We are not to expect that men who paid ſo little regard to their charter in matters of religion, would adhere to it further than was conſiſtent with the great object in view in matters of polity. So far as it promoted their independence, they complied with its directions, but no further. They eſtabliſhed a popular government conformable to it. But inſtead of governing the ſociety by the general ſtatute and common law of the realm, or conforming to the principles of thoſe laws in ſuch as were made

by

by themſelves, they enacted new laws totally repugnant to, and ſubverſive of, them. Although the charter gave them no authority over the life of the ſubject, they aſſumed and conferred it on their courts of judicature. And it was a ſettled opinion, that the laws of England had no force in their ſociety, unleſs brought over and confirmed by their own legiſlature. They formed a new code of laws, founded on the laws of Moſes, much more ſevere, and in many inſtances more ſanguinary, than either the ſtatute or common law. Their laws were extended to facts committed out of the juriſdiction of their corporation, and their courts took cogniſance of piracies, murders, felonies, and other offences committed on the high ſeas, while the laws of England made for the regulation of their commerce were utterly diſregarded. A law for the puniſhment of ſedition or treaſon, or any offence againſt the perſon of the King, or againſt the ſtate, was not known in their ſociety. And it is remarkably characteriſtic of this people, that although they made proviſion againſt the perpetration of every other crime which human nature is liable to commit, and particularly one to puniſh treaſon againſt their own government with death, this only ſhould be wanting in their firſt ſyſtem of polity. This circumſtance, added to the popular form of their government, their diſlike to the Engliſh laws, and their inſtitution of a code ſo totally different, are ſo many proofs, amounting to demonſtration, of their diſaffection to the Crown, their enmity to mixed monarchy, and of their fixed reſolution to eſtabliſh an independent commonwealth of their own.

Under this charter the people of Maſſachuſſett's remained until it was reſumed by Charles II. A few years after the Prince of Orange arrived, and the Revolution in England took place, fond of their old licentiouſneſs and confuſed government, they petitioned in vain for a renewal of their old charter. That wiſe prince, little acquainted as he muſt have been with the conſtitution of England, ſaw its defects, and wiſhed, by a new one, to bring back thoſe people to a juſt attachment to the Government he intended to ſupport. This is evident from the alterations he made; but whether it was occaſioned by the critical ſituation of his affairs in England, or to ſome other cauſe, it is certain he did not lay the axe to the root. Some of the former popular rights were lopped off, but, like pruning the exterior branches of a tree, they only tended to ſwell and ſtrengthen the trunk. They did not eradicate the ſpirit of their Moſaical laws; they did not eſtabliſh that balance, and thoſe checks on the licentious power of the people, which are neceſſary under a mixed Government.

The governor, under the new charter, is appointed by the Crown; he has a power to adjourn, prorogue, or diſſolve the aſſembly—his aſſent is neceſſary to all laws—he has the ſole appointment of military officers. Theſe were all amendments of the old charter, and tended to bring their Government a little nearer in reſemblance to that of the State; but the reſemblance was very imperfect and diſtorted; for ~~the deputy governor is~~

yet

~~yet chosen by the people, and~~ the governor cannot appoint any of the officers of the courts of justice without the assent of the council. All other civil officers are elected by the two houses, while he only retains a negative on their choice; and the council, who are thus united with him in his executive powers, are chosen or appointed by the general court or assembly. Thus the first branch of the legislature is deprived of the occasional, and often necessary, assistance and weight of the second; and the executive power is bound in the chain of democratical influence in such manner, that it cannot appoint a single officer of Government without the assent of a popular assembly. The second branch, which ought to be unbiassed and independent, is the creature of the people, and dependent on them for their annual existence; while the third or democratical branch, besides all the powers necessary to check the excess of authority in the governor, possess a considerable share in the royal rights and prerogatives of the Crown. In this truly injudicious and absurd manner are the principles of the three simple forms of government jumbled together. Instead of three branches uninfluenced by, and independent of, each other in their judgments and decisions, the two highest in order, and most dignified, are dependent on the lowest and meanest.

It would extend these observations to a tedious length, should I give a circumstantial detail of all the ambitious designs and arbitrary attempts made by the assemblies of this Province, from time to time, to render the two other branches of the legislature yet more dependent, and to assume all power into their own hands. I shall therefore only mention some of them, referring my reader to the History wrote by Governor Hutchinson, who appears to be the best informed of any of their historians.

It is an essential part of the English constitution, that the King should be independent; that the civil list should be fixed and permanent, and the expence and support of the Crown should not depend on the annual vote of the other branches of the legislature. It is for the same reason just and necessary, that Governors of Provinces should have reasonable and independent salaries for the support of their dignity and freedom of judgment; but the assemblies of the Massachussett's, in order to deprive the governor of the free exercise of his judgment in the administration of government, have ever refused to grant a fixed salary. Their grants have been only from year to year, or half-yearly; they have been withheld or granted according as the governor gratified them in all their popular measures and designs; and in some instances, by this means, they have compelled their governors to violate their instructions, and submit to acts equally injurious to the rights of the Crown, and the true interest of the people.

The history and public records of the Province afford a variety of attempts of the assembly to assume all the powers of the Crown, and to render their Governor and Council cyphers in government. They will prove, that their assemblies have assumed a right to appoint officers, who by the directions of the charter can only be appointed by the general court; that they have

have of their own authority embodied and arrayed men in arms, and ſent them upon expeditions, contrary to the judgment, and againſt the will of the governor; that they have interfered with his right to treat with the natives, and prevented a treaty; that they have aſſumed the ſuperintendence of his Majeſty's armies, forts and garriſons; that they have undertaken to iſſue proclamations, and to appoint illegal and arbitrary committees, and to order the Attorney-General to carry on illegal proſecutions; that they have aſſumed the right of adjourning their houſe againſt the will and conſent of the King's repreſentative, in whom alone that right was veſted by the charter; that they have attempted to appoint the council without conſent of the governor, and when appointed, to deprive them of their eſſential rights; that they have paſſed a vote for removing the general court to a different place from that appointed in the governor's writ; that they have attempted to deprive him of his right, by the charter, to draw on the treaſury for the ordinary exigencies of Government; that they have attempted to take upon themſelves the command and direction of the militia; that they have compelled their governor to give up the right of treating with the natives, to treat in the name of the general court, and to ſubmit to their inſpection the very ſpeech he was about to make to them; that they have attempted to aſſume the powers of a court-martial, and appointed committees to take the ſole conduct of the war with the natives out of the governor's hands; that they have threatened to draw off the forces by their own authority from the

the defence of the Province; that they have taken from the governor his right to pay the officers of government, and ſuffer no draughts on the treaſury for payment of the ſalaries of officers, until the aſſembly have judged of the performance of their ſervices; that they have refuſed to pay a military officer his wages, becauſe he had obeyed the orders of the governor, agreeable to military duty; and that they have paſſed a reſolve that the governor's public ſeal, affixed to a meſſage delivered to the Indians, be defaced.

After theſe ſpecimens of the turbulent and ſeditious conduct of the people of this Province, *educated under the unlimited and unconſtitutional powers of their former and preſent charter*, and that too during their feeble and infant ſtate, we are naturally led to look forward to meaſures more alarming to Government, as ſoon as they ſhall be poſſeſſed of greater numbers and more ſtrength. But before we proceed to unfold thoſe meaſures, we muſt, for the ſake of having all the original cauſes of ſo great a rebellion before us, take a view of the other charters granted to promote the ſettlement of America. In theſe we ſhall find the ſame deviations from the form of the principal government, the ſame unlimited and unconſtitutional powers, and conſequently, in the people educated under them, the ſame popular averſion and ſeditious oppoſition to the laws and conſtitution of the Britiſh State, and the ſame deſign of becoming, as ſoon as their ſtrength and maturity would enable them, an independent people.

The charters I allude to, are thoſe of Rhode-Iſland and Connecticut. Theſe charters, upon com-

comparing them with that of Maſſachuſſetts, will be found in no reſpect eſſentially different. The form of their government was in ſubſtance the ſame. All the legiſlative, executive, and even the fœderative powers, or the rights of war and peace, were veſted in the freemen of the province. They were ſo many pure democracies, without the leaſt mixture of ariſtocracy or monarchy. All thoſe checks, and that balance of power, which form the excellence of the Britiſh government, and which give it ſtrength, and ſecure the freedom of its ſubjects, were omitted. They were in fact conſtituted by their ſeveral charters ſo many complete independent ſocieties, eſtabliſhed within the ſtate. I call them independent, becauſe in tenure as well as extent of power, they were ſo unlimited, that nothing was wanting which could be neceſſary to a ſociety perfectly independent.

The inferior corporations of the Engliſh ſociety, and I may add, of all other ſocieties whatever, are formed on the polity of their principal ſyſtems. They are governed by the general laws of the ſtate; in Great Britain by the common and ſtatute laws; and their legiſlative powers are ſo confined, that they have often occaſion to apply to the ſupreme authority for laws and local regulations neceſſary to their own particular welfare. It is this, which in part forms the ſubordination and dependence of all inferior politic bodies. But theſe ſocieties were made competent to every act which could be neceſſary in a ſociety perfectly independent. There was no one regulation which could be neceſſary to their intereſt

 or

or happineſs, for which they were obliged to look up to or aſk of the Parliament. And what is yet more extraordinary, all ſuperintendence over their legiſlative, executive, or fœderative powers, was given up by the ſupreme repreſentative of the ſtate. They were not obliged to tranſmit any of their tranſactions for the inſpection or controul either of the Crown or Parliament. They made what laws they pleaſed, and executed them in what manner they pleaſed, and made peace and war with whom they pleaſed. Under theſe circumſtances, if they were not independent, they were certainly, in more ſenſes of the word than one, unaccountable communities, and ſuch as never were formed within the authority of any other government hitherto known in the hiſtory of mankind. They were what the learned Puffendorf calls "*irregular and monſtrous ſtates within a ſtate* *.

Under thoſe charters the people of Rhode Iſland and Connecticut received their education. Their political as well as their religious princi-

* This Author, in treating of inferior ſocieties, ſays, "With regard to lawful bodies, it is to be obſerved, that "whatever *right* they poſſeſs, or whatever *power* they hold "over their members, is all under the *determination of the* "*ſupreme authority*, which it ought on no account to *oppoſe* "or overbalance. For otherwiſe, if there could be a body "of men, not *ſubject to the regulations of the civil govern*-"*ment*, there would be a *ſtate within a ſtate*." And ſpeaking of the right of the "ſupreme governor" to form ſuch ſocieties, he further ſays, "If he has given in expreſs words, "*an abſolute and independent right* with regard to *ſome par*-"*ticular affairs*, which concern the *public adminiſtration*, "then he hath plainly ABDICATED his authority, and by "admitting *two heads* in the conſtitution, hath rendered it "*irregular and monſtrous*."

ples

ples became fixed. Both were equally popular, and both tended to erase every sentiment in favour of mixed monarchy. All the fundamental laws upon which the structure of the State had been erected, were at one stroke abolished by the institution of a democracy; and not a single principle remained which could remind them of the excellence or value of the government to which they were or ought to be subordinate. Such was the education of British subjects in these two colonies, which in no essential respect, either in their religion or polity, differed from that of the Massachussetts Government.

The influence and different effects of education on the principles, manners, affections, and prejudices of men, are to be seen in every department of life; in every private family; in every private and public school and college; and in every different system of government. "Train up a child in the way he should go, "and when he is old he will not depart from "it," is a sacred precept, as necessary to be observed in politics, as in religion or morality, and was undoubtedly intended to be so by its author. The fundamental and general laws of every society are the lessons of instruction, by which the subject is daily taught his duty and mode of obedience to the State. It is the uniformity of these lessons, flowing from the same system of consistent polity, which forms the same habits, manners, and political opinions throughout the society, fixes the national attachment, and leads the people to look up to one system of government for their safety

and

and happineſs, and to act in concert on all occaſions to maintain and defend it.

The force of this national attachment, thus fixed by an habitual ſubmiſſion to the ſame ſyſtem of government and laws, is to be ſeen in the conduct of every ſociety, where the uniformity of its ſyſtem is preſerved. We ſee it equally powerful in a monarchy, a republic, or a mixed government. Will a Frenchman change the abſolute power of his King, a Spaniard the deſpotiſm of his Monarch, or a Turk the tyranny of his Baſhaw, for the civil rights of a Briton? He will not, becauſe habit here becomes a ſecond nature. It compels him to love his oppreſſion, and to prefer it to reaſonable liberty. Uſe has rendered it not only tolerable, but preferable, in his opinion, to that freedom which is founded in different polity, and which he knows not how to aſſume.

In ſocieties, founded on principles ſo repugnant to thoſe of the Britiſh government, it is reaſonable to expect that a faction would be formed, ever watchful to ſeize the firſt opportunity of throwing off the ſmall remains of ſubordination to the State. Such a faction did exiſt, as I have ſhewn, from their firſt ſettlement, waiting for the opportunity with much ſolicitude and impatience. Many difficulties prevented the attempt. For a great length of time they were in an infant ſtate, and incompetent in numbers. Their frequent quarrels and wars with the Indians kept them employed, haraſſed, and diſtreſſed. The neighbourhood of the Canadians, and the deſigns of France, which led

to

to a conqueſt of their country, and the arrival of people from Great Britain, of different principles, with regard both to religion and government, were ſo many obſtacles to their deſign.

At the concluſion of the laſt war, the two principal difficulties were removed. The ceſſion of Canada to Great Britain at once diſpelled their dread of Indian and Canadian incurſions, and their numbers were greatly increaſed, which left them at leiſure to execute their dark and inſidious deſign of revolting from the parent ſtate, under whoſe wing they had been tenderly nurſed and protected. Nothing now was wanting, but a plan for collecting their ſtrength, and forming an union of thoſe in the different parts of America, who they imagined might be moſt eaſily brought into the meaſure. The Preſbyterians in the ſouthern colonies were the people with whom they wiſhed to be united. The religious and political principles of theſe ſectaries, they knew, would eaſily aſſimilate with their own; for, beſides other reſemblances, they acknowledged no temporal head to their churches, claiming rights uncontroulable by the civil authority; and their ideas of government were equally popular.

The New England Congregationaliſts, under their firſt charter, had held their ſynods. They again, in the year 1725, attempted it under their ſecond, and obtained the Lieutenant Governor's aſſent to the meaſure. But this attempt being laid before the Lords Juſtices, they were forbid to proceed in it. The prohibition was certainly a wiſe one. It could not be prudent to ſuffer men, who had ſo often cruelly perſecuted, not only the members of the eſtabliſhed church, but of every other ſociety differing in opinion from them, and who held principles ſo dangerous to the eſtabliſhed conſtitution of the State, to meet in a public body, and in an authoritative manner, without the conſent of the King, who in all ſound policy ought to be the head of every public body, whether civil or religious. But undiſmayed at this check to their intended union, they never reſted until they had eſtabliſhed it in ſubſtance, though under a different name. Inſtead of a ſynod, they called it a committee. In this committee they were as effectually united as they could have been in a ſynod. They exerciſed the ſame powers, and were a ſynod in every thing but the name.

The churches of the Preſbyterians throughout the Colonies had hitherto remained unconnected with each other. To form theſe into one religious, as well as one political body, and to eſtabliſh an alliance with them, was therefore the firſt meaſure purſued by this congregational faction, after they found themſelves freed from the embarraſſments and dangers of Indian and French incurſions.

This meaſure was accelerated by the reſolution of the Houſe of Commons to lay certain duties in America on ſtamped paper, in the year 1763. It was neceſſary for them to become able to give effectual oppoſition to the intention of Parliament, if it ſhould paſs into an Act. Diſperſed over the Colonies, diſunited among themſelves, and diſliked and ſuſpected as they were by people of all other perſuaſions of religion, they deſpaired of ſucceſs, while it depended

pended on their own ſtrength. It was therefore recommended to all the Preſbyterians in the Colonies ſouthward of New England, to form themſelves into one body. A meaſure ſo flattering to their vanity and love of power was adopted without heſitation.

In the beginning of the year 1764, a convention of the miniſters and elders of the preſbyterian congregations in Philadelphia wrote a circular letter to all the preſbyterian congregations in Pennſylvania, and with it incloſed the propoſed articles of union. The reaſons aſſigned in them are ſo novel, ſo futile, and abſurd, and the deſign of exciting that very rebellion, of which the congregationaliſts of New England, and the Preſbyterians in all the other Colonies are at this moment the only ſupport, is ſo clearly demonſtrated, that I ſhall make no apology for giving them to the Reader at full length, without any comment.

The Circular Letter and Articles of "ſome Gentle-" men of the Preſbyterian Denomination," in the Province of Pennſylvania.

"SIR, *Philadelphia, March* 24, 1764.

"The want of union and harmony among "thoſe of the preſbyterian denomination has "been long obſerved, and greatly lamented by "every public-ſpirited perſon of our ſociety. "Notwithſtanding we are ſo numerous in the "province of Pennſylvania, we are conſidered "*as nobody*, or a body of very little weight and "conſequence, ſo that any encroachments upon "our *eſſential* and *charter privileges* may be

H "made

" made by evil-minded persons, who think " that they have little to fear from *any opposi-* " *tion* that can be made to their measures by " us. Nay, some denominations openly insult " us as acting without plan or design, quarrel- " ling with one another, and seldom uniting to- " gether, even to promote the most salutary " purposes: And hence they take occasion to " misrepresent and asperse the whole body " of Presbyterians, on the account of the " indiscreet conduct of individuals belonging " to us. It is greatly to be wished that we " could *devise some plan* that would cut off even " the least grounds for such aspersions, that " would enable us to prevent the bad conduct " of our members, and that would have a ten- " dency *to unite us more closely together*; so that, " *when there may be a necessity to act as a body*, " we may be able to do it whenever we may " be called *to defend our civil or religious liberties* " *and privileges*, which we may enjoy, or to " obtain any *of which we may be abridged.*

" A number of gentlemen in this city, in " conjunction *with the clergymen* of our deno- " mination here, have thought that the enclosed " Plan may be subservient to this *desirable pur-* " *pose*, if it be heartily adopted and prosecuted " by our brethren in this province, and three " lower counties; and in this view we beg " leave to recommend it to you. It cannot " possibly do any hurt to us, and it will beyond " doubt make us a more *respectable body*. We " therefore cannot but promise ourselves your " hearty concurrence from your known public " spirit, and desire to assist any thing that may

" have

" have a tendency to promote the *union and* " *welfare of society*, and the general good of the " community, *to which* WE *belong*.

" We are your's, &c."

The PLAN *or* ARTICLES.

" Some gentlemen of the presbyterian deno" mination, having seriously considered the ne" cessity of *a more close union among ourselves*, in " order to enable us to act *as a body with una*" *nimity and harmony*, &c. have unanimously " adopted the following plan, viz.

" 1st, That a few gentlemen in the city of " Philadelphia, with the ministers of the pres" byterian denomination there, be chosen to " correspond with their friends in different " parts, to *give and receive advices, and to con*" *sult what things may have a tendency to promote* " *our union and welfare, either as a body*, or, as " we are connected together in particular con" gregations, as far as it will consist with our " duty to the best of Kings, and our subjection " to the laws of Government.

" 2d, That a number of the most prudent " and public-spirited persons in each district in " the province, and three lower counties, be " chosen, *with the ministers* in said districts, to " correspond in like manner with one another, " and with the gentlemen appointed for this " purpose in Philadelphia; or,

" 3d, That the same be done in each con" gregation or district where there is no mi" nister; a neighbouring minister meeting

" with them as oft as is convenient and ne-" ceſſary.

" 4th, That a perſon ſhall be appointed in " each committee thus formed, who ſhall ſign " a letter in the name of the committee, and " to whom letters ſhall be directed, who ſhall " call the committee together, and communi-" cate to them what advice is received, that " they may conſult together what is beſt to be " done.

" 5th, That one or more members be ſent by " the committee in each county or diſtrict, " yearly or half-yearly, to a *general meeting of* " *the whole body*, to conſult together what is " neceſſary for the advantage of the body, and " to give their advice in any affairs that relate " to particular congregations; and that one " ſtated meeting of ſaid delegates be on the laſt " Tueſday of Auguſt yearly.

" 6th, That the place of the general meeting " be at Philadelphia or Lancaſter, on the laſt " Tueſday of Auguſt, 1764.

" 7th, That each committee tranſmit to the " committee in Philadelphia, their names and " numbers, with what alterations may at any " time be made in them.

" 8th, That the committee in town conſiſt of " miniſters of the preſbyterian denomination " in this city, and Mr. Treat, together with

Meſſ. Samuel Smith
Alex. Huſton
George Brian
John Allen
William Alliſon
H. Williamſon

Meſſ. T. Montgomery
Andrew Hodge
John Redman
Jed. Snowden
Iſaac Snowden
Robert Harris

Meff. Thomas Smith	Meff. Wm. Humphrys
Sam. Purviance	John Wallace
John Meafe	J. Macpherfon
H. M'Cullough	John Bayard
P. Chevalier, jun.	John Wikoff
Ifaac Smith	William Ruft
Charles Petit	S. Purviance, jun.
William Henry	

In confequence of this letter, an union of all the prefbyterian congregations immediately took place in Pennfylvania and the Lower Counties. A like confederacy was eftablifhed in all the fouthern Provinces, in purfuance of fimilar letters wrote by their refpective conventions. Thofe letters were long buried in ftudied fecrecy. Their defign was not fufficiently matured, and therefore not proper for publication. Men of fenfe and forefight were alarmed at fo formidable a confederacy, without knowing the ultimate extent of their views; however, at length, in the year 1769, the letters from the conventions of Philadelphia and New-York were obtained and publifhed.

An union of prefbyterian force being thus eftablifhed in each Province, thefe projectors then took "*falutary fteps*" (as they are called in a letter from one of the committee at Philadelphia to his friend) to get the whole "prefbyterian intereft on the *Continent* more firmly united." Thefe fteps ended in the eftablifhment of an annual Synod at Philadelphia. Here all the prefbyterian congregations in the Colonies are reprefented by their refpective minifters and elders. In this fynod all their general affairs, political

political as well as religious, are debated and decided. From hence their orders and decrees are iſſued throughout America; and to them as ready and implicit obedience is paid as is due to the authority of any ſovereign power whatever.

But they did not ſtop here: the principal matter recommended by the faction in New England, was an union of the *congregational and preſbyterian intereſt* throughout the Colonies. To effect this, a negociation took place, which ended in the appointment of a ſtanding committee of correſpondence, with powers to communicate and conſult, on all occaſions, with a like committee appointed by the congregational churches in New England. Thus the Preſbyterians in the ſouthern Colonies, who, while unconnected in their ſeveral congregations, were of little ſignificance, were raiſed into weight and conſequence; and a dangerous combination of men, whoſe principles of religion and polity were equally averſe to thoſe of the eſtabliſhed Church and Government, was formed.

United in this manner throughout the Colonies, theſe republican ſectaries were prepared to oppoſe the Stamp Act, before the time of its commencement; and yet ſenſible of their own inability without the aid of others, no arts or pains were left uneſſayed to make converts of the reſt of the people; but all their induſtry was attended with little ſucceſs. The members of the Church of England, Methodiſts, Quakers, Lutherans, Calviniſts, Moravians, and other diſſenters, were in general averſe to every meaſure

ſure which tended to violence. Some few of them were, by various arts and partial intereſt, prevailed on to unite with them; and theſe were either lawyers or merchants, who thought their profeſſional buſineſs would be affected by the act, or the bankrupt planters, who were overwhelmed in debt to their Britiſh factors. But the republicans, pre-determined in their meaſures, were unanimous. It was theſe men who excited the mobs, and led them to deſtroy the ſtamped paper; who compelled the collectors of the duties to reſign their offices, and to pledge their faith that they would not execute them; and it was theſe men who promoted, and for a time enforced, the non-importation agreement; and by their perſonal applications, threats, inſults, and inflammatory publications and petitions, led the aſſemblies to deny the authority of Parliament to tax the Colonies, in their ſeveral remonſtrances.

The effect of theſe meaſures was a repeal of the act. This repeal had its conſequences, but they were the reverſe of thoſe expected by Government. It had been better for both countries that it never had paſſed, or never been repealed. The authority of Parliament had been denied, the political incompetency of the Colonies to grant their reaſonable proportion of aids had been experienced. At the ſame time the duty and ability of the Colonies to contribute towards the national defence was acknowledged, the Miniſter, whoſe ambition and folly had obtained the repeal, had condeſcended to give the moſt diſgraceful aſſurances, that the right in Parliament to tax the Colonies, affirmed by the Declaratory

claratory Act, would never be exercised. All these were so many circumstances, which could not fail to elate the seditious republicans, and to convince them if they persevered, they would ultimately succeed in their design.

Had Government, instead of repealing the act, and passing the Declaratory Bill, suffered the act to remain in force until they had digested and adopted the measure, which has been since proposed for removing the great objection upon which the opposition was founded, it would have prevented the rebellion at least for the present. The plausible pretext of seeking a redress from unconstitutional taxation, by which many were deluded into the opposition, could not have been made; the people in general would have been satisfied, and the republican faction must have surceased, or suspended their opposition to Government; but the minister of that day was not the minister of wisdom, suppose it were possible to believe him the minister of integrity.

Encouraged by this repeal, the factions in America were not idle. They daily expected, notwithstanding ministerial assurances, that some other act would pass for compelling the Colonies to support the expence of their own Governments, and to contribute to the national safety. They expected it, because it was just; but determined not to submit to it, they were constantly active in forming the minds of the people for opposition. No art, no fraud, no falsehood, by which they could be misled, was omitted; their fears and their ambition were alternately worked upon. In the New England papers the flattering idea that "*America would ſoon become a great empire,*" was repeatedly held out to the people. It was ſaid that the *corner ſtone was already laid*; and a variety of artful arguments were uſed to lead the vanity of the people to that belief. Some publications denied the authority of Parliament over the Colonies in all caſes whatever; others charged the Britiſh legiſlature with corruption, the Miniſters with an inſidious deſign to enſlave America; and even the mildeſt of Sovereigns, *who never yet has violated the royal covenant with his people in any one inſtance,* did not eſcape their petulant reproaches.

While theſe things were tranſacting in America, the act for *laying duties on certain goods imported into the Colonies*, was paſſed in Britain. The faction who were thus on their watch, and determined to oppoſe not only every act for taxing the Colonies, but every one that ſhould be made to bind them, inſtantly took the alarm.

There was another deſcription of men whoſe intereſt was affected by it: theſe were the ſmuggling merchants in the ſea-port towns, who in defiance of law and the moſt ſacred of all obligations, an oath, had been long in the practice of importing tea from St. Euſtatia and Holland. Theſe men joined the republicans in their clamours againſt the act; but if their clamours were heard, they were diſregarded by the people in general; who ſaw that the act was not founded in oppreſſion, but on the contrary was greatly beneficial.

Encouraged by this diſpoſition in the people, and the acquieſcence of the colonial aſſemblies under the partial repeal of the act, the Parliament paſſed another to enable the Eaſt-India Company to export their teas to America. This act, I have before obſerved, was a favour to the people of America, who therefore, in general, did not oppoſe it; but it affected the intereſt of the ſmuggler yet more eſſentially than the Tea Act; and it was another inſtance of the exerciſe of parliamentary authority over the Colonies, which the republicans were determined, at all events, to oppoſe. The united faction of Congregationaliſts, Preſbyterians, and Smugglers, took the alarm, and renewed their exertions to create a general inſurrection; but they did not ſucceed.

The people in general ſuſpected the independent views of the republicans; they ſaw the intereſted motives of the ſmugglers, and they knew the regulations in the act were beneficial to themſelves; they were therefore not to be moved. The faction now, giving over all hope of aſſiſtance from the country, reſolved to prevent the landing of the tea; becauſe if not landed it would not be bought, and could not be conſumed; and if landed they knew, from the evident diſpoſition of the people, that it would be impoſſible to prevent either the ſale or conſumption. For this reaſon, in all the ſea-port towns they again formed themſelves into committees, and prepared to execute their deſign.

On the arrival of the tea, every fiction and phantom of oppreſſion were held up to the view

of

of the people, in all the towns where it was expected, in order to lead them into mobs for its destruction. It never has been a difficult matter in any country, and more especially in those where liberty prevails, to incite the ignorant and necessitous vulgar, by false pretences, to acts of violence. It has not been so in London; it was not so in America. Mobs were raised in every port where the tea arrived, and the landing was prevented in all, except Charles Town; and in Boston it was violently, and in defiance of law, destroyed.

Had that firmness, that intrepidity of spirit, which ever is the greatest ornament and support of public justice, and which ever was necessary to preserve the peace in a great empire, prevailed in the British Councils, an exemplary punishment would have been inflicted on every city and town where such open and rebellious opposition had been given to the supreme authority of the State. But this was not the case. The disunion in the great Councils of the State, and the factious opposition to Government, even at that early period, encouraging the rising sedition, smothered the ideas of public justice, and wrenched the sword from the hands of Government. No punishment was inflicted, nor was any reprehension given to those cities which had seditiously opposed the authority of Parliament by their obstructions to the landing of the tea; and even that which was imposed on the port of Boston could not be called a punishment, unless it be one to restore that which we have unlawfully and violently taken from another. This act, with that for altering the Massachussett's charter, which I have before taken notice of, were added to the list of American grievances.

While these mild measures, these temporary and inadequate expedients, were taking by Government to support the authority of the State, the factions on both sides of the Atlantic were not idle. The republicans in America had their spies, their friends, and their parties in Britain. From the time of the Stamp Act, and its disgraceful repeal, every measure was taken to unite them more firmly together; and this was no difficult task. Ingredients of the same quality will easily assimilate. The views of both were the same. The first had in prospect the independence of America—the second, the abolition of the principles of mixed monarchy in Britain: and both wished to establish their respective societies on democratical principles. To effect this union, the particular lords and commoners, through whose influence the repeal had been obtained, had received the most fulsome letters of adulation and thanks from the American demagogues, and had returned their answers, which plainly discovered they were pleased with their *new allies*. Letters of the same kind were written to the factious and republican corporations in Britain, which had signalised themselves in the American cause. The city of London was at their head. A correspondence was moreover settled with many other principal republicans in all parts of the kingdom, and even in Ireland.

These seditious combinations being thus united, have constantly acted in concert. They have, with assiduity unparalleled, and exertions

incessant,

incessant, promoted each others designs. That in Great Britain has constantly received all the inflammatory letters, resolves, and proceedings of the American town meetings, committees, conventions, and congresses, which were equally calculated to deceive and delude the people of both countries, and to lead them into rebellion. It has industriously published and transmitted those letters and resolves throughout the kingdom, with publications of its own equally inflammatory. It has, by harangues, paragraphs, and pamphlets (I wish speeches, even in the two houses of parliament, could be excepted), been the constant and firm support of every act of American sedition. And the greatest and most cautious man among them had the boldness to declare in a British senate, "that he "rejoiced that America had resisted."

On the other side, the American rebel committees have been favoured with the constant communications of the faction in Britain, whose seditious speeches in parliament, petitions, pamphlets, and publications, have been constantly transmitted and published in America to increase the sedition, and push that unhappy people into the present most unprovoked, groundless, and destructive rebellion. A collection of all these inflammatory pieces would fill a volume in folio. They have been, and are to be seen in the British and American papers and pamphlets; and they are transactions so recent, that they need not be particularly pointed out.

The Assemblies of the several Colonies, and the people in general, from the time of the partial repeal of the Tea Act, remained quiet and unmoved

unmoved by these seditious publications. The Assemblies (those of the Charter-Colonies excepted) were not to be influenced by party writings, and inflammatory pieces. They knew they were members of the British Government. They knew the necessity of a supreme legislative authority in every State; and they saw that Great Britain, unmoved at their former indiscreet petitions, denying the supreme authority of the State, was determined to support it. They knew their own incompetency to discharge with justice the first of all political duties, the granting of aids for the common safety of the empire. They also saw, that a Parliament in which they were not represented, in which no person and no property in America was represented; a parliament which had no constitutional means of knowing their wants, necessities, and circumstances, in order to regulate their conduct or to relieve their wants, was not so competent in reason, however it might be in law, to bind them. They saw the Colonies in the same situation with Wales, Durham, and Chester before their representation in Parliament; and therefore, like them, they wished for a more perfect union with the British State. They also saw that it was their duty to propose and petition for the measure which would relieve them from their perplexing situation. But they did not, nor could know each other's minds. They were thirteen disunited bodies, as incompetent to this measure as to that of granting their just proportion of the national aids, and the faction abroad added to their perplexities. In this doubtful state they remained until

until a circular letter ſent to the Speakers of all the Aſſemblies was received by ſuch as were ſitting, from that ſource of ſedition, a committee of correſpondence appointed by the Aſſembly of the Maſſachuſetts.

The meaſure propoſed by this letter was a general non-importation and non-exportation between Great Britain and America, a meaſure which one would not ſuſpect could poſſibly be recommended by any man in Great Britain; and yet we know, that it was not only recommended, but vindicated and ſupported by the whole tribe of pretended patriots. Many letters were written from Great Britain, recommending it. An extract from one of them, wrote even by a member of P———t, publiſhed in the Pennſylvania Gazette, is in a ſtyle ſo truly republican and rebellious, that I will give it to the Reader in its own words. "I perſuade myſelf "your countrymen are not ſo contaminated "with the effeminacy of this nation, not to ſee "that this is the *important criſis* when they "ought to make a *ſolemn*, *ſullen*, *united*, and "*invincible ſtand* againſt the *cruel*, *tyrannous*, "and *ruinous ſyſtem of policy* adopted and exer-"ciſing by this legiſlature, againſt the rights "and freedom of America; and let me add, "that if the *deputies of the ſeveral Provinces*, "when convened in Congreſs, do not, *one and* "*all*, firmly reſolve to eſtabliſh, through "every county and townſhip in their reſpective "Provinces, a ſolemn league and covenant, "and under an *oath or affirmation* not to pur-"chaſe or to uſe the manufactures of this coun-"try (ſave what are collected already within the "Province),

" Province), and if poſſible not to export *any* " *proviſions to the Weſt India Iſlands*, and at the " ſame time do not *religiouſly reſolve to meet* " *again in Congreſs once in every ſix months*, for " the purpoſe of forming a ſuitable plan for " ſecuring American rights and freedom, *our* " *children* will be irremediably deprived of that " inheritance of liberty which *our* forefathers " carefully and *piouſly* tranſmitted to us."

The Aſſemblies, which were the conſtitutional repreſentatives of the people of the Colonies, and which well knew the general ſenſe of their conſtituents, ſaw the dangerous tendency of this meaſure, that it could not fail to irritate the mother country, and bring on the people they repreſented her juſt indignation and vengeance. And moreover, they knew that a meaſure of this kind could not be carried into execution, but by illegal conventions, committees, town-meetings, and their ſubſervient mobs, which would ſoon put an end to all order, and deſtroy the authority of Government. They ſaw that this was the deſign and ultimate wiſh of the Boſtonian faction and their Britiſh colleagues; and therefore ſuch as had an opportunity, and even the committees of thoſe who had not, recommended the only meaſure which had the leaſt probability of preventing it. They recommended a Congreſs to be compoſed of delegates from the ſeveral aſſemblies, who knew that the people in general were not diſaffected to the Britiſh Government, and that they wiſhed to be more firmly united with it upon conſtitutional principles. From theſe convened in a general council, they hoped that ſome propoſitions would be made, which would terminate in a perfect accommodation and union between the two countries, and that the views of the republicans would be frustrated, which they dreaded yet more than what they thought was an unconstitutional power in parliament. And their hopes would have been answered, had the measure been carried into complete execution; that is, had the delegates in congress been appointed by the assemblies of the several colonies. But this was prevented by the injudicious conduct of some of the royal Governors, who, disapproving of the measure, did not give their assemblies an opportunity of appointing their delegates. This irritated even some of those who were friendly to Government, and it left to the republican faction the choice of men who thought as they thought, and would act as they wished. In the Colonies where the assemblies had an opportunity of meeting, they chose the delegates; where they had not, they were chosen by the illegal and factious conventions, committees, and town-meetings. Thus the Congress was of a motley complexion, partly loyalists, and partly republicans.

The Congress met at Philadelphia in September, 1774. They brought with them their appointments and instructions. The latter plainly discover the dispositions of the assemblies, and of the people who gave them, and demonstrate their aversion to every thing which might tend to a seditious or illegal opposition to Government. They strictly enjoined their delegates to "pursue *proper*,

" *prudent, and lawful measures,* and to adopt a " plan for obtaining a redress of American " grievances, ascertaining American rights up- " on the most solid and *constitutional* principles, " and for establishing that union and harmony " between Great Britain and the Colonies, " *which is indispensably necessary to the welfare and* " *happiness of both.*" Under these instructions, it was the general expectation that decent petitions would be presented to Parliament, explicitly pointing out the measures by which its authority over the Colonies might be rendered more constitutional, and the grievances complained of might be redressed; because this was nothing more than the reasonable duty of subjects, and it was the sincere wish of the people.

Upon the meeting of Congress, two parties were immediately formed, with different views, and determined to act upon different principles. One intended candidly and clearly to define American rights, and explicitly and dutifully to petition for the remedy which would redress the grievances justly complained of—to form a more solid and constitutional union between the two countries, and to avoid every measure which tended to sedition, or acts of violent opposition. The other consisted of persons, whose design, from the beginning of their opposition to the Stamp Act, was to throw off all subordination and connexion with Great-Britain; who meant by every fiction, falsehood and fraud, to delude the people from their due allegiance, to throw the subsisting Governments into anarchy, to incite the ignorant and vulgar to arms, and with those arms to establish American Independence. The one were men of loyal principles, and possessed the greatest fortunes in America;, the other were congregational and presbyterian republicans, or men of bankrupt fortunes, overwhelmed in debt to the British merchants. The first suspected the designs of the last, and were therefore cautious; but as they meant to do nothing but what was reasonable and just, they were open and ingenuous. The second, fearing the opposition of the first, were secret and hypocritical, and left no art, no falsehood, no fraud unessayed to conceal their intentions. The loyalists rested, for the most part, on the defensive, and opposed, with success, every measure which tended to violent opposition. Motions were made, debated and rejected, and nothing was carried by either.

While the two parties in Congress remained thus during three weeks on an equal balance, the republicans were calling to their assistance the aid of their factions without. Continual expresses were employed between Philadelphia and Boston. These were under the management of Samuel Adams—a man, who though by no means remarkable for brilliant abilities, yet is equal to most men in popular intrigue, and the management of a faction. He eats little, drinks little, sleeps little, thinks much, and is most decisive and indefatigable in the pursuit of his objects. It was this man, who by his superior application managed at once the faction in Congress at Philadelphia, and the factions in New England. Whatever these patriots ni Congress wished to have done by their colleagues without, to induce General Gage, then at the head of his Majeſty's army at Boſton, to give them a pretext for violent oppoſition, or to promote their meaſures in Congreſs, Mr. Adams adviſed and directed to be done; and when done, it was diſpatched by expreſs to Congreſs. By one of theſe expreſſes came the inflammatory reſolves of the county of Suffolk, which contained a complete declaration of war againſt Great-Britain. By theſe reſolves it is declared, "that no obedience is due to acts of Parliament affecting Boſton:"

That "the juſtices of the ſuperior courts of judicature, court of aſſize, &c. are unconſtitutional officers, and that no *regard ought to be paid to them by the people*:"

That "the county will ſupport and bear harmleſs all ſheriffs and their deputies, conſtables, jurors and other officers, who ſhall *refuſe to carry into execution the orders of the ſaid courts*:"

That "the collectors of taxes, conſtables and other officers, retain in their hands *all public monies*, and not make any payment thereof to the provincial county treaſurer:"

And that "the perſons who had accepted ſeats at the council-board, by *virtue of a mandamus from the King*, ſhould be conſidered as *obſtinate and incorrigible enemies to their country*."

They adviſe the people "to elect the officers of militia, and to uſe their *utmoſt diligence to acquaint themſelves with the art of war* as ſoon as poſſible, and for that purpoſe to appear under arms once in every week:"

And to carry theſe and other meaſures into execution; among many other things equally treaſonable,

treaſonable, they recommend it to the ſeveral towns to "chuſe a Provincial Congreſs."

Upon theſe reſolves being read, a motion was made that the Congreſs ſhould give them their ſanction. Long and warm debates enſued between the parties. At this time the republican faction in Congreſs had provided a mob, ready to execute their ſecret orders. The cruel practice of tarring and feathering had been long ſince introduced. This leſſened the firmneſs of ſome of the loyaliſts; the vote was put and carried. Two of the diſſenting members preſumed to offer their proteſt againſt it in writing, which was negatived. They next inſiſted that the tender of their proteſt and its negative ſhould be entered on the minutes; this was alſo rejected.

By this treaſonable vote the foundation of military reſiſtance throughout America was effectually laid. The example was now ſet by the people of Suffolk, and the meaſure was approved of by thoſe who called themſelves *the repreſentatives of all America.* The loyal party, although they knew a great majority of the coloniſts were averſe to the meaſure, perceived the improbability of ſtemming the torrent. They had no authority, no means in their own power to reſiſt it; they ſaw thoſe who held the powers of Government inactive ſpectators, and either ſhrinking from their duty, or uniting in the meaſures of ſedition; they ſaw the flame of rebellion ſpreading with more rapidity in a province under the eye of his Majeſty's army than in any other; and that no effectual meaſures were taking by Government in Britain to ſup-

preſs

press it; and yet, as a petition to his Majesty had been ordered to be brought in, they resolved to continue their exertions. They hoped to prevail in stating the rights of America on just and constitutional principles; in proposing a plan for uniting the two countries on those principles, and in a clear, definitive and decent prayer, to ask for what a majority of the colonies wished to obtain; and as they had no reason to doubt the success of this measure in a British Parliament, they further hoped, that it would stop the effusion of blood and the ruin of their country.

With this view, as well as to probe the ultimate design of the republicans, and to know with certainty whether any proposal, short of the absolute independence of the Colonies, would satisfy them, a plan of union was drawn by a member of the loyal party, and approved by the rest. It was so formed as to leave no room for any reasonable objection on the part of the republicans, if they meant to be united to Great Britain on any grounds whatever. It included a restoration of all their rights, and a redress of all their grievances, on constitutional principles; and it accorded with all the instructions given to them as members of Congress.

Introductory to his motion which led to this plan, the author of it made, in substance, the following speech, which is taken from his short notes: " He told Congress that he came with " instructions to propose some mode, by which " the harmony between Great Britain and the " Colonies might be restored on constitutional " principles: that this appeared to be the

" genuine

" genuine ſenſe of all the inſtructions brought " into Congreſs by the Delegates of the ſeveral " Colonies. He had long waited with great " patience under an expectation of hearing ſome " propoſition which ſhould tend to that ſalutary " and important purpoſe; but, to his great " mortification and diſtreſs, a month had been " ſpent in fruitleſs debates on equivocal and " indeciſive propoſitions, which tended to in- " flame rather than reconcile—to produce war " inſtead of peace between the two countries. " In this diſagreeable ſituation of things he " thought it his incumbent duty to ſpeak " plainly, and to give his ſentiments without " the leaſt reſerve.

" There are," ſays he, " two propoſitions " before the Congreſs, for reſtoring the wiſhed- " for harmony: one, that Parliament ſhould " be requeſted to place the Colonies in the ſtate " they were in in the year 1763; the other, " that a non-exportation and non-importation " agreement ſhould be adopted. I will con- " ſider theſe propoſitions, and venture to reject " them both; the firſt, as indeciſive, tending to " miſlead both countries, and to lay a founda- " tion for further diſcontent and quarrel; the " other, as illegal, and ruinous to America.

" The firſt propoſition is indeciſive, becauſe " it points out no ground of complaint—aſks " for a reſtoration of no right, ſettles no prin- " ciple, and propoſes no plan for accommo- " dating the diſpute. There is no ſtatute which " has been paſſed to tax or bind the Colonies " ſince the year 1763, which was not founded " on precedents and ſtatutes of a ſimilar nature

" before

" before that period; and therefore the pro-
" position, while it expressly denies the right
" of Parliament, confesses it by the strongest
" implication. In short, it is nugatory, and
" without meaning; and however it may serve,
" when rejected by Parliament, as it certainly
" will be, to form a charge of injustice upon,
" and to deceive and inflame the minds of the
" people hereafter, it cannot possibly answer any
" other purpose.

" The second proposition is undutiful and
" illegal: it is an insult on the supreme autho-
" rity of the State; it cannot fail to draw on the
" Colonies the united resentment of the Mother
" Country. If we will not trade with Great
" Britain, she will not suffer us to trade at all.
" Our ports will be blocked up by British men
" of war, and troops will be sent to reduce us
" to reason and obedience. A total and sudden
" stagnation of commerce is what no country
" can bear: it must bring ruin on the Colonies:
" the produce of labour must perish on their
" hands, and not only the progress of industry
" be stopped, but industry and labour will
" cease, and the country itself be thrown
" into anarchy and tumult. I must therefore
" reject both the propositions; the first as in-
" decisive, and the other as inadmissible upon
" any principle of prudence or policy.

" If we sincerely mean to accommodate the
" difference between the two countries, and to
" establish their union on more firm and con-
" stitutional principles, we must take into con-
" sideration a number of facts which led the
" Parliament to pass the acts complained of,

" since

" ſince the year 1763, and the real ſtate of the " Colonies. A clear and perfect knowledge of " theſe matters only can lead us to the ground " of ſubſtantial redreſs and permanent har- " mony. I will therefore call your recollection " to the dangerous ſituation of the Colonies " from the intrigues of France, and the incur- " ſions of the Canadians and their Indian allies, " at the commencement of the laſt war. None " of us can be ignorant of the juſt ſenſe they " then entertained of that danger, and of their " incapacity to defend themſelves againſt it, " nor of the ſupplications made to the Parent " State for its aſſiſtance, nor of the cheerfulneſs " with which Great Britain ſent over her fleets " and armies for their protection, of the millions " ſhe expended in that protection, and of the " happy conſequences which attended it.

" In this ſtate of the Colonies, it was not " unreaſonable to expect that Parliament would " have levied a tax on them proportionate to " their wealth, and the ſums raiſed in Great " Britain. Her ancient right, ſo often exer- " ciſed, and never controverted, enabled her, " and the occaſion invited her, to do it. And " yet, not knowing their wealth, a generous " tenderneſs ariſing from the fear of doing " them injuſtice, induced Parliament to for- " bear to levy aids upon them—It left the " Colonies to do juſtice to themſelves and to " the nation. And moreover, in order to " allure them to a diſcharge of their duty, it " offered to reimburſe thoſe Colonies which " ſhould generouſly grant the aids that were " neceſſary to their own ſafety. But what was "the conduct of the Colonies on this occasion, "in which their own existence was immediately "concerned? However painful it may be for "me to repeat, or you to hear, I must remind "you of it. You all know there were Colo- "nies which at some times granted liberal aids, "and at others nothing; other Colonies gave "nothing during the war; none gave equitably "in proportion to their wealth, and all that "did give were actuated by partial and self- "interested motives, and gave only in proportion "to the approach or remoteness of the danger. "These delinquencies were occasioned by the "want of the exercise of some supreme power "to ascertain, with equity, their proportions of "aids, and to over-rule the particular passions, "prejudices, and interests, of the several "Colonies.

"To remedy these mischiefs, Parliament "was naturally led to exercise the power which "had been, by its predecessors, so often exer- "cised over the Colonies, and to pass the "Stamp Act. Against this act the Colonies "petitioned Parliament, and denied its autho- "rity. Instead of proposing some remedy, by "which that authority should be rendered "more equitable and more constitutional over "the Colonies, the petitions rested in a decla- "ration that the Colonies could not be repre- "sented in that body. This justly alarmed the "British Senate. It was thought and called by "the ablest men and Britain, a clear and ex- "plicit declaration of American Independence, "and compelled the Parliament to pass the "Declaratory Act, in order to save its ancient

"and

" and incontrovertible right of ſupremacy over " all the parts of the empire. By this inju- " dicious ſtep the cauſe of our complaints " became fixed, and inſtead of obtaining a " conſtitutional reformation of the authority of " Parliament over the Colonies, it brought on " an explicit declaration of a right in Parlia- " ment to exerciſe abſolute and unparticipated " power over them. Nothing now can be " wanting to convince us, that the Aſſemblies " have purſued meaſures which have produced " no relief, and anſwered no purpoſe but a bad " one. I therefore hope that the collected " wiſdom of Congreſs will perceive and avoid " former miſtakes; that they will candidly and " thoroughly examine the real merits of our " diſpute with the Mother Country, and take " ſuch ground as ſhall firmly unite us under " one ſyſtem of polity, and make us one " people.

" In order to eſtabliſh thoſe principles, upon " which alone American relief ought, in reaſon " and policy, to be founded, I will take a " brief view of the arguments on both ſides of " the great queſtion between the two countries— " a queſtion in its magnitude and importance " exceeded by none that has been ever agitated " in the councils of any nation. The advo- " cates for the ſupremacy of Parliament over " the Colonies contend, that there muſt be one " ſupreme legiſlative head in every civil ſociety, " whoſe authority muſt extend to the regulation " and final deciſion of every matter ſuſceptible " of human direction; and that every member " of the ſociety, whether political, official, or

 " individual,

"individual, muſt be ſubordinate to its ſupreme "will, ſignified in its laws: that this ſupremacy and ſubordination are eſſential in the "conſtitution of all States, whatever may be "their forms; that no ſociety ever did, or "could exiſt, without it; and that theſe truths "are ſolidly eſtabliſhed in the practice of all "Governments, and confirmed by the concurrent "authority of all writers on the ſubject of "civil ſociety.

"Theſe advocates alſo aſſert, what we cannot "deny—That the diſcovery of the Colonies "was made under a commiſſion granted by the "ſupreme authority of the Britiſh State, "that they have been ſettled under that au- "thority, and therefore are truly the pro- "perty of that State. Parliamentary juriſdic- "tion has been conſtantly exerciſed over them "from their firſt ſettlement; its executive "authority has ever run through all their in- "ferior political ſyſtems: the Coloniſts have "ever ſworn allegiance to the Britiſh State, and "have been conſidered, both by the State and "by themſelves, as ſubjects of the Britiſh Go- "vernment. Protection and allegiance are reci- "procal duties; the one cannot exiſt without the "other. The Colonies cannot claim the pro- "tection of Britain upon any principle of reaſon "or law, while they deny its ſupreme autho- "rity. Upon this ground the authority of "Parliament ſtands too firm to be ſhaken by "any arguments whatever; and therefore to "deny that authority, and at the ſame time to "declare their incapacity to be repreſented,

" amounts to a full and explicit declaration of " independence.

" In regard to the political ſtate of the Co- " lonies, you muſt know that they are ſo many " inferior ſocieties, diſunited and unconnected " in polity. That while they deny the authority " of Parliament, they are, in reſpect to each " other, in a perfect ſtate of nature, deſtitute " of any ſupreme direction or deciſion what- " ever, and incompetent to the grant of na- " tional aids, or any other general meaſure " whatever, even to the ſettlement of differences " among themſelves. This they have repeatedly " acknowledged, and particularly by their " delegates in Congreſs in the beginning of the " laſt war; and the aids granted by them ſince " that period, for their own protection, are a " proof of the truth of that acknowledg- " ment.

" You alſo know that the ſeeds of diſcord " are plentifully ſowed in the conſtitution of " the Colonies; that they are already grown to " maturity, and have more than once broke " out into open hoſtilities. They are at this " moment only ſuppreſſed by the authority of " the Parent State; and ſhould that authority " be weakened or annulled, many ſubjects of " unſettled diſputes, and which, in that caſe, " can only be ſettled by an appeal to the ſword, " muſt involve us in all the horrors of civil " war. You will now conſider whether you " wiſh to be deſtitute of the protection of Great " Britain, or to ſee a renewal of the claims of " France upon America; or to remain in our " preſent diſunited ſtate, the weak expoſed to

" the

" the force of the ſtrong. I am ſure no honeſt man " can entertain wiſhes ſo ruinous to his country.

" Having thus briefly ſtated the arguments " in favour of parliamentary authority, and " conſidered the ſtate of the Colonies, I am " free to confeſs that the exerciſe of that " authority is not perfectly conſtitutional in " reſpect to the Colonies. We know that the " whole landed intereſt of Britain is repreſented " in that body, while neither the land nor the " people of America hold the leaſt participation " in the legiſlative authority of the State. Re- " preſentation, or a participation in the ſupreme " councils of the State, is the great prin- " ciple upon which the freedom of the Britiſh " Government is eſtabliſhed and ſecured. I " alſo acknowledge, that that territory whoſe " people have no enjoyment of this privilege, " are ſubject to an authority unreſtrained and " abſolute; and if the liberty of the ſubject " were not eſſentially concerned in it, I ſhould " reject a diſtinction ſo odious between mem- " bers of the ſame ſtate, ſo long as it ſhall be " continued. I wiſh to ſee it exploded, and " the right to participate in the ſupreme " councils of the State extended, in ſome form, " not only to America, but to all the Britiſh " dominions; otherwiſe I fear that profound " and excellent fabrick of civil polity will, ere " long, crumble to pieces.

" The caſe of the Colonies is not a new one. " It was formerly the very ſituation of Wales, " Durham, and Cheſter.

" As to the tax, it is neither unjuſt nor op- " preſſive, it being rather a relief than a bur-

" then;

" then; but it is want of constitutional principle " in the authority that passed it, which is the " ground for complaint. This, and this only, " is the source of American grievances. Here, " and here only, is the defect; and if this defect " were removed, a foundation would be laid " for the relief of every American complaint; " the obnoxious statutes would of course be " repealed, and others would be made, with " the assent of the Colonies, to answer the same " and better purposes; the mischiefs arising " from the disunion of the Colonies would be " removed; their freedom would be established, " and their subordination fixed on solid con-" stitutional principles.

" Desirous as I am to promote the freedom " of the Colonies, and to prevent the mischiefs " which will attend a military contest with Great " Britain, I must intreat you to desert the " measures which have been so injudiciously " and ineffectually pursued by antecedent As-" semblies. Let us thoroughly investigate the " subject matter in dispute, and endeavour to " find from that investigation the means of " perfect and permanent redress. In whatever " we do, let us be particular and explicit, and " not wander in general allegations. These " will lead us to no point, nor can produce any " relief; they are besides dishonourable and " insidious. I would therefore acknowledge " the necessity of the supreme authority of " Parliament over the Colonies, because it is a " proposition which we cannot deny without " manifest contradiction, while we confess that " we are subjects of the British Government;

" and

" and if we do not approve of a reprefentation " in Parliament, let us afk for a participation " in the freedom and power of the Englifh " conftitution in fome other mode of incor- " poration; for I am convinced, by long " attention to the fubject, that let us deliberate, " and try what other expedients we may, we " fhall find none that can give to the Colonies " fubftantial freedom, but fome fuch incorpo- " ration. I therefore befeech you, by the " refpect you are bound to pay to the inftruc- " tions of your conftituents, by the regard you " have for the honour and fafety of your " country, and as you wifh to avoid a war with " Great Britain, which muft terminate, at all " events, in the ruin of America, not to rely on " a denial of the authority of Parliament, a " refufal to be reprefented, and on a non- " importation agreement; becaufe whatever " proteftations, in that cafe, may be made to " the contrary, it will prove to the world, that " we intend to throw off our allegiance to the " State, and to involve the two countries in all " the horrors of a civil war.

" With a view to promote the meafure I " have fo earneftly recommended, I have pre- " pared the draught of a plan for uniting Ame- " rica more intimately, in conftitutional polity, " with Great Britain. It contains the great " outlines or principles only, and will require " many additions in cafe thofe fhould be ap- " proved. I am certain, when difpaffionately " confidered, it will be found to be the moft per- " fect union in power and liberty with the " Parent State, next to a reprefentation in

" Parliament, and I truſt it will be approved " of by both countries. In forming it, I have " been particularly attentive to the rights of " both; and I am confident that no American, " who wiſhes to continue a ſubject of the Britiſh " State, which is what we all uniformly profeſs, " can offer any reaſonable objection againſt it.

" I ſhall not enter into a further explanation " of its principles, but ſhall reſerve my ſen- " timents until the ſecond reading, with which " I hope it will be favoured."

The introductory motion being ſeconded, the Plan was preſented and read. Warm and long debates immediately enſued on the queſtion, Whether it ſhould be entered in the proceedings of Congreſs, or be referred to further conſideration. All the men of property, and moſt of the ableſt ſpeakers, ſupported the motion, while the republican party ſtrenuouſly oppoſed it.

The queſtion was at length carried by a majority of one Colony.

I ſhall not preſent the reader with the Plan. It has been laid before the Houſe of Commons, and publiſhed in Mr. Galloway's Examination. It will ſuffice here to obſerve, that it propoſed an American branch of the Britiſh legiſlature to be eſtabliſhed in America, and incorporated with the Parliament for the purpoſes of American taxation, and other general regulations. In this branch every Colony would have been repreſented more perfectly than the people of Great Britain are in Parliament; and no law to bind America could be made without her conſent, given by her repreſentatives; and yet the republican faction, having obtained a majority in Congress by their arts, and the assistance of their mobs, rejected it without suffering it to be discussed, contrary to their own positive rule; and ordered it to be expunged from their minutes, to prevent its publication.

I have dwelt more particularly on the conduct of the Congress relative to this plan, because their denial of the authority of Parliament, their refusal to be represented in it, and their rejecting a proposition which would have given the Colonists a perfect representation in America; a representation by far more popular and perfect than that in Great Britain, are so many concurrent and incontestible proofs which must carry conviction to every candid breast, that they have, from the beginning, aimed at nothing short of absolute independence.

It has been the constant theme of the factions on both sides of the Atlantic, that at the conclusion of the last war a "plan for enslaving "the Colonies was concerted, and has ever "since been pertinaciously carrying into execu-"tion, by the present administration." It has been echoed from one country to another a thousand times. It has been refuted again and again, and rests now as it did at first, having nothing but the boldness and insolence of rebellion to support it: for the truth is, that "at "the conclusion of the last war," the New England demagogues, educated under their democratical charter, in principles inimical to a mixed monarchy, found themselves, by the cession of Canada to Great Britain, relieved from the burthens and embarrassments arising from their

their continual wars with the Canadians and Indians. They thought that the Colonies thus relieved, and now grown up to confiderable ftrength, no longer ftood in need of the protection of Great Britain; that the time was approaching when they might carry into execution their long meditated defign of eftablifhing their own religion and popular governments in America.

A variety of facts and tranfactions might be adduced to demonftrate this truth. Prior to this æra, they had ever recognifed the jurifdiction of Parliament. Statutes were made for regulating their trade, levying taxes, reftraining their manufactures, and directing their internal police; to all which they fubmitted without murmur or complaint. But immediately fubfequent to this period, their doctrine was changed, and a new fyftem of conduct was adopted. It was in the beginning of the year 1764, before the Stamp Act was thought of, and before they pretend that they had any grievances to complain of, that they began their unlawful combinations, "to defend (as they exprefsly declare) their civil and religious liberties." It was in the fame year that they refolved to unite all the prefbyterian churches throughout America, before that time unconnected with each other, into one body or fynod; and to combine that fynod with the great committee at Bofton, by ftanding committees, appointed to correfpond and confult with each other. It was at this time they began to hold out to the people the novel, but alluring idea, of American independence. And it was at this time

 they

they declared, that the *corner ſtones* (meaning the ceſſion of Canada, and the eſtabliſhment of their union) were laid; and that America would ſoon riſe to a *great independent empire*. This declaration was followed by many publications tending to alienate the affections of the people from the Mother Country, and to prepare them, as the Congreſs expreſſed it, "for future events." And it was in the ſame year, for the firſt time, that they laid the foundation for quarrel, by a denial of the ſupreme authority of Great Britain.

In the year 1764, the Stamp Act was paſſed. It paſſed without one diſapproving voice. The men in the preſent oppoſition to Government had given it their approbation. They had not then formed a connection with rebellion, nor had they compared their notes with the American republicans; but as ſoon as the rebels in America took the ground of oppoſition, the two factions inſtantly embraced, and the ſame men who had in 1764 aſſented to the act, in 1766 became the moſt violent oppoſers of it, and of every other ſubſequent act which has paſſed for the ſupport of the ſupreme authority of their own country over its Colonies.

It may be both amuſing and inſtructive to the reader, and not foreign to my purpoſe, to lay before him a copy of General *Conway*'s excellent letter to the Governor of Maſſachuſſett's Bay, in 1765. Though the General wrote officially, being one of his Majeſty's principal Secretaries of State, yet if he was governed by any principles of honour or honeſty, his own ſentiments muſt have correſponded with the letter.

"It

"It is with the greatest concern (says he), " his Majesty learns the disturbances which " have lately arisen in your Province, the gene- " ral confusion that seems to reign there, and " the total languor and want of energy in your " Government to exert itself with any dignity " or efficacy, for the suppression of tumults " which seem to strike at the very *being of all* " *authority and subordination amongst you.*

"Nothing can certainly exceed the ill-advised " and intemperate conduct held by a party in " your Province, which can in no way con- " tribute to the removal of any real grievance " they might labour under, but may tend to " impede and obstruct the exertion of his Ma- " jesty's benevolent attention to the ease and " comfort, as well as to the welfare of all his " people.

"It is hoped and expected, that this want " of confidence in the justice and tenderness of " the Mother Country, and this open resistance " to its authority, can only have found place " among the lower and more ignorant of the " people: the better and wiser part of the " Colonies will know, that decency and sub- " mission may prevail, not only to redress " grievances, but to obtain grace and favour, " while the *outrage of a public violence can expect* " *nothing but severity and chastisement.*

"These sentiments you and all his Majesty's " servants, from a sense of your duty to, and " love of your country, will endeavour to ex- " cite and encourage; you will, in a particular " manner, call upon them, not to render their " case desperate. You will in the strongest

" colours

" colours represent to them, the dreadful con-
" sequences that must inevitably attend the
" *forcible and violent resistance to acts of the British*
" *Parliament*, and the scene of misery and de-
" struction to *both countries inseparable from such*
" *a conduct*.

" For however unwillingly his Majesty may
" consent to the exertion of such powers as may
" endanger the *safety of a single subject*; yet
" can he not permit his own dignity and the
" authority of the British legislature to be tram-
" pled on by force and violence, and in avowed
" contempt of all order, duty and decorum.

" If the subject is aggrieved, he knows in
" what manner *legally and constitutionally to apply*
" *for relief*; but it is not suitable either to the
" safety or dignity of the British empire, that
" any individuals, under the pretence of re-
" dressing grievances, should *presume to violate*
" *the public peace*."

Such were the sentiments of Mr. Conway, Secretary of Sate. What has been his conduct as member of Parliament, and how far it has corresponded with those sentiments since he has united with Opposition, and with them become the advocate of the Americans, his and their speeches in the great councils of the State have fully demonstrated.

In this opposition, it is remarkable how much they have been embarrassed to find arguments, even plausible, to support themselves. They have been led to make distinctions the most absurd and ridiculous—distinctions which are to be found in no book, nor in the constitution of any Government, and which they themselves have either forgot, or are now ashamed any longer to insist

 on.

on. Not daring to deny the ſupremacy of Parliament over the Colonies in all caſes whatſoever, they have contended, there is a diſtinction between the rights of legiſlation and taxation—between the right to impoſe internal and external taxes—and taxes laid for the regulation of trade, and thoſe for the purpoſe of revenue; and that Parliament was competent to the firſt, but not to the ſecond. Thus endeavouring, by their ſophiſtry, to pare away, or ſplit into pieces, the ſupreme authority of the State, and to rob it of the moſt important of its rights, by which only it can command the reaſonable contributions of all its ſubjects when neceſſary to the national defence.

Such are the facts, upon which I ſhall appeal to the reader's deciſion, whether there is any evidence of a deſign in Government, ſince the concluſion of the laſt war, to enſlave the Colonies; or whether there are not the ſtrongeſt proofs that human conduct can exhibit, that from that period there has exiſted a ſettled deſign in the republican Coloniſts to throw off their allegiance to the State, and in their Britiſh colleagues to encourage and ſupport them in their attempt.

Many other facts might be adduced in ſupport of the ſame truths; but I will not dwell upon matters which are ſufficiently proved, and which perhaps ſome men may think a digreſſion. I will therefore diſmiſs the Britiſh, and paſs to the American faction, which I left after their rejection of the only propoſal which was made tending to an accommodation of the diſpute between the two countries.

tries. They next proceeded to ſettle their Bill of Rights. In this bill, were there no other proof of their deſign to eſtabliſh independence, we ſhould find that which is abundantly ſufficient. Their fourth reſolve declares, that "as "the Engliſh Coloniſts *are not* repreſented, "and from their local circumſtances, *cannot* "properly be repreſented in the Britiſh Parliament, they are intitled to a FREE AND EXCLUSIVE *power of legiſlation* in their ſeveral "provincial legiſlatures in all caſes of *taxation* "and *internal polity*, ſubject only to the negative "of their ſovereign." Now no words can convey a more explicit declaration of colonial independence on parliamentary authority; for if the Colonies are not, and will not be repreſented, and moreover have a *free* and excluſive power of legiſlation in all caſes of *taxation and internal polity*, the authority of the Britiſh legiſlature is perfectly excluded; becauſe it can make no law which muſt not come within the deſcription of this reſolve, not even an act to regulate their trade; for that muſt be executed by officers within the Colonies, and of courſe muſt affect their *internal polity*. It cannot even repeal a colonial law, however repugnant to the laws of England, or injurious to the intereſt of the other parts of the empire.

If ſo explicit a declaration can require any thing to confirm its meaning, we ſhall find it in the following words of the ſame reſolve. "But "from the neceſſity of the caſe, and a regard "to the mutual intereſt of both countries" (not from any conſtitutional right of Parliament, for this is denied in the preceding part of the reſolve),

" resolve) we consent to the operations of" (not to the right of making) " such acts of the " British Parliament as are" (not to such as *shall be*) " *bona fide* restrained to the regulation of " our external commerce, for the purpose of " securing the commercial advantages of the " whole empire to the Mother Country, and the " commercial benefits of its respective mem- " bers." Thus did these mén assume a right to declare all the laws of trade void in respect to America, to judge of the propriety and utility of all, to refuse obedience to by far the greater part, and, with an arrogance unparalleled, to give validity to such of them only as they pleased.

Such was the complexion of the Bill of Rights. They next proceeded to consider an address to his Majesty, for they would not condescend to call it a petition. Perhaps they thought they could not, with propriety, call it so, as it did not ask for any one essential thing. The loyalists, and friends to an union between the two countries, zealously contended that it was equivocal and indecisive; that it asked for nothing; that it was moreover calculated to incense and irritate his Majesty and his Parliament, rather than to obtain a redress of grievances; that the Colonists had always acknowledged themselves subjects of the British State, and truly were so; that it was their duty not only to point out their grievances, but clearly and explicitly to ask for a remedy; that therefore the address ought to contain the great principles of the dispute, and to propose some mode of relief; and that commissioners should be ſent over to Britain to ſolicit the redreſs propoſed. One may ſafely affirm that theſe arguments were juſt, and the force of them ought to have prevailed, ſince they urged nothing more than was the reaſonable duty, and invariable practice of good ſubjects. But reaſon or argument had little weight. The republican faction had obtained, by working upon the timidity of ſome, and the ignorance of others, a majority. The addreſs was therefore carried as it was brought in, with ſome very trifling amendments.

Upon a view of this addreſs, what does it pray for? There is, indeed, an intimation (if an intimation may be called a prayer) that if the Parliament will repeal the ſtatutes ſince the year 1763, their complaints will *ſubſide*. The word *ſubſide* was prudently and cautiouſly choſen. It alluded to atoms at the bottom of a fluid, ready to riſe at the leaſt emotion; and this would have been the caſe had the Parliament complied with this intimation. For they had prepared and ſettled other complaints, or, as they ſtyled them, oppreſſions, as grounds of future quarrel and war between the two countries, as ſoon as the ſtatutes made ſince the year 1763 ſhould be repealed. They had declared their excluſive right of legiſlation, and had denied the force of all the laws of trade; and of every ſtatute paſſed before that period, on the principles eſtabliſhed by their claim of rights. The right of parliament to make them was as expreſsly denied, as it was to paſs thoſe ſince 1763; and it was their fixed reſolution to make theſe ſtatutes the ſubject of diſſention as

ſoon

ſoon as the Coloniſts were better ſtrengthened, and prepared for war.

To ſupport this fact, the unprejudiced Reader cannot look for ſtronger proof than their own ſolemn declarations. Theſe are the completeſt evidence of deſigns not carried into execution. They muſt carry conviction to the human breaſt, where reaſon and candour are not excluded. On theſe then I rely. In a clauſe of their claim of rights, on which their addreſs was founded, they declare, that "in the courſe "of their enquiry, they find *many* infringe- "ments and violations of the foregoing rights, "*which they paſs over* FOR THE PRESENT, and "proceed to ſtate ſuch acts and meaſures as "have been adopted *ſince the laſt war*." And in another clauſe, ſpeaking of the ſtatutes, they add, "To theſe grievous acts and meaſures "Americans cannot ſubmit," and therefore "they have, *for the preſent* ONLY, reſolved to "purſue the following *peaceable* meaſures: "1ſt, To enter into a non-importation, non- "conſumption, and non-exportation agreement; "2d, To prepare an addreſs to the people of "Great Britain, and a memorial to the inha- "bitants of the Britiſh Colonies; and 3d, To "prepare a loyal addreſs to his Majeſty." How far from peaceable theſe meaſures were, let common ſenſe judge. The firſt was carried into execution by every act of violence that lawleſs committees and deſperate mobs could deviſe. The ſecond was calculated to inflame the minds of the people againſt their ſovereign, and to raiſe another rebellion in Britain. The third, to incite the people of America to take up arms againſt their mother country, and to prepare their minds (as it is expreſſed) "for mournful "events, and every contingency." The addreſs, intimating that their complaints would ſubſide upon the repeal of the ſtatutes ſince 1763, was ſent over and preſented; but their reſolves reſpecting the preceding objects of their complaints, and their determination to take them up at a future day, were ſecreted, not only from Britons, but Americans.

This conduct was artful, treacherous, and baſe, in reſpect to both countries. It was equally calculated to amuſe and deceive both. But it was abſolutely neceſſary to the ſucceſsful purſuit of their dark and treaſonable deſign, which they knew would be reliſhed by the greater part of neither. At this time they were deſtitute of every thing neceſſary for military reſiſtance. They had not formed their ſtanding committees, conventions, or congreſſes in the ſeveral Colonies. They had not embodied themſelves in arms. They had not diſarmed the diſaffected, nor had they in the country arms or ammunition neceſſary to their deſign.

Amuſement, falſehood, and fraud, were therefore the only means they then had. Theſe were to be improved into weapons of more effect and power. Their colleagues in faction on this ſide of the Atlantic were to be ſupported, becauſe they were neceſſary to diſtract the councils of ſtate, and retard its meaſures. The people of America, then more happy than any other on the globe, were to be duped into

 rebellion.

rebellion. To effect these purposes, dissimulation was necessary; and never, not even by the Cromwellian faction, was more of it used than on this occasion. In all their public proceedings, whether meant to delude the people of Great Britain or of America, we find the most solemn declarations of loyalty to the King, the most ardent desire of a connection and union on constitutional principles with Great Britain, a solemn disavowal of independence, and the strongest asseverations that their sole design was to obtain a redress of American grievances; and all this at the very time they were making every possible preparation for the most vigorous hostile opposition.

Having taken this plausible ground, they transmitted their proceedings to the faction in Britain. A vote of congressional thanks to "those truly *noble, honourable, and patriotic advocates*, who had so generously and powerfully, though unsuccessfully, espoused and defended the cause of America, both in and out of parliament," attended them. A letter was written to their agents, ordering them to advise and co-operate with all "great men who might incline to aid the cause of liberty and mankind." Their memorial to the people of Great Britain was ordered to be "communicated particularly to all the trading cities and manufacturing towns in Great Britain." And their agents were constituted so many spies on the British Government, with orders to give the "earliest information of all such conduct

"and

" and deſigns of miniſtry or parliament, as " might concern America to know."

The ſyſtem of ſeditious oppoſition, in both countries, to the meaſures of Government, being thus concerted, the Congreſs broke up. The loyaliſts ſeeing no hope of oppoſing the approaching ſtorm, retired to their families. The republicans adjourned to a tavern, in order to concert the plan which was neceſſary to be purſued by their party, throughout the Colonies, for raiſing a military force. This ſettled, they alſo returned to their reſpective Colonies.

And here the two parties acted upon very different principles. The loyalty of the firſt forbad them to join in the ſedition, and taught them to look up to Government to take the lead in ſuppreſſing it. But they ſoon found that the powers of the colonial governments were inſulted with impunity, and were daily giving way to new uſurpations, without any exertion to prevent it. However, they hoped that the time was approaching, when the powers of the State would be exerted; and they knew, that thoſe powers, if conducted with wiſdom, would be more than ſufficient to cruſh the intended rebellion. But the republicans were well appriſed that they muſt riſe into power by their own induſtry. They were therefore indefatigable throughout America. The diſcontented and factious were convened in every Colony. Provincial congreſſes, conventions, and committees of ſafety were appointed by a part of the people in every diſtrict, which, when compared with the whole, was truly inconſiderable. Theſe illegal bodies hav-

ing

ing elected men of the most seditious principles, for members of the next Congress, proceeded to other business.

The loyalists were disarmed, the most obnoxious of them imprisoned.. The loyal presses were restrained, some of them seized and destroyed. Publications in favour of Government were publicly burnt, while the republican presses teemed with speeches of their friends and allies in parliament, and letters wrote from their colleagues in faction in England, with a thousand other literary performances, all tending to lead the people into a rebellious opposition to Government. Every measure that art and fraud could suggest, as necessary to delude the people into arms, was industriously pursued. All the Gunsmiths were employed in the manufacturing of musquets; warlike stores of every kind were sent for to foreign countries; the militia in New England became embodied, in pursuance of the recommendation of the Suffolk resolve, and magazines of warlike stores were laid up to be ready for their use. To seize one of these magazines General Gage sent out a party, which was attacked by the militia at Lexington.

On the 10th of May the second Congress met, and a circular letter from the American agents, calculated to persuade the Colonists that no relief was to be obtained from Government, was laid before them. On the same day the Boston delegates delivered a letter from the Provincial Congress of their Colony, informing, that they had resolved to raise an army of 13,600 men, and to borrow 100,000

pounds

pounds towards their ſupport; and that they had made propoſals to the Congreſs of New-Hampſhire, Rhode-Iſland, and Connecticut, for furniſhing men in the ſame proportion. On the 16th, advice was received by the Preſident, that a detachment from the Maſſachuſſett's and Connecticut militia had taken his Majeſty's fort at Ticonderoga.

While theſe matters were before them, the reſolution of the Houſe of Commons of February 20th, 1775, tranſmitted to Governor Franklin, and by him laid before the aſſembly of New-Jerſey, was by that aſſembly ſubmitted to their conſideration. This reſolution was made upon the ground the Americans had taken. They had repeatedly confeſſed that a grant of their reaſonable proportion of aids was their indiſpenſable duty; their aſſemblies had been repeatedly called upon for that purpoſe; their grants had been untimely, partial, and unjuſt; and ſome, when called on, in times of the greateſt danger, either neglected or refuſed a compliance with the requiſition. They had moreover denied the authority of Parliament, and refuſed to be repreſented in it. Upon this ground, Parliament could offer nothing more liberal towards the Colonies than this propoſition.

The propoſition amounts to this: *The Colonies have declared that they are willing to grant their reaſonable proportion of aids for the common defence, and to provide for their reſpective civil eſtabliſhments; now if the Colonies will propoſe to do this by their ſeveral legiſlatures, and if ſuch propoſal ſhall appear to be juſt, and be approved*

of

of by his Majeſty, and the two Houſes of Parliament, ſo long as ſuch propoſals ſhall be carried into effect, Parliament ſhall forbear, in reſpect to the Colony complying, to levy any duty, tax, or aſſeſſment, except only the duties neceſſary for the regulation of commerce; and even the nett proceeds of theſe duties ſhall be carried to the account of the Colony complying with the propoſal. In this propoſition, what was it that Parliament reſerved? They gave up the mode of raiſing and levying the taxes, to the colonial aſſemblies: and to remove all poſſibility of inducement in Parliament to draw a revenue from them under the pretence of regulating their commerce, they declare that the revenue thus raiſed, ſhall be carried to the credit of their national aids. The only power reſerved is leſs than was ever before reſerved by the ſupreme authority of any State whatever; and it is no more, when candidly examined, and ſtripped of the falſe colours with which the Congreſs has bedaubed it, than a right to compel a Colony to do juſtice to the community of which it is a member; and that not before it has given proof of its diſobedience and non-compliance with its firſt and moſt important duty. Such a power all men muſt acknowledge is eſſential to their ſubordination, to their union, to their protection and ſafety. It muſt therefore be lodged ſomewhere. And where could it be more properly, or more ſafely placed, than in the ſupreme authority of the State?

Now if the Colonies are members of the Britiſh State—if they will not be repreſented in Parliament—if they have no ſupremacy among themſelves to aſcertain their proportion of aids, or to compel them to make their reaſonable contributions, which are all facts acknowledged by themſelves; and if they have not propoſed, or aſked, for the eſtabliſhment of any means by which the State may have a ſecurity, that they will, when their own ſafety and that of the nation are in danger, perform their reaſonable duty, was Parliament to continue to protect them with the monies levied on the people of Great-Britain, and to give up all power of compelling them to grant their reaſonable proportions? If they intended that the Britiſh Parliament ſhould have any authority over them at all, what leſs *could it retain?* If they did not approve of this propoſition, and did not mean to be abſolutely independent, why did they not propoſe the means by which they might be dependent, agreeable to the conſtitution they ſo much admired? If they had any other union of the two countries, more conſtitutional, in view, why did they not petition for it? Their inſtructions ordered them to do ſo—it was the earneſt wiſh of the generality of their conſtituents. Why then did they not comply with thoſe inſtructions, if they diſliked the propoſition? I call upon the factions on both ſides of the Atlantic; the voice of reaſon and juſtice unites with me in the call, to aſſign any other reaſon why they neither made this propoſition a ground of accommodation, nor propoſed to Parliament any other, but that they were determined, through all the horrors attendant on rebellion, to eſtabliſh their independence.

Reſolved to avoid every path to a reconciliation with Great-Britain, becauſe inconſiſtent with their views of independence, they rejected this propofition as " unreafonable and infidious," and proceeded with the utmoft induftry in their military preparations. Were I to give a minute relation of them, it would be attended with a prolixity which no entertainment to be derived from them could compenfate. I fhall therefore only mention in general, the principal meafures which they thought neceffary to be eftablifhed, before they could fafely declare their long meditated independence. They appointed a committee to provide magazines of ammunition and military ftores. They abolifhed the general poft-office eftablifhed by act of Parliament, and inftituted another. They declared the offices of Governor and Lieutenant-Governor of Maffachuffett's vacant, and recommended to the people of that Province to inftitute a new Government. They refolved to raife a regular army. They appointed the commander in chief, and other officers, and ordered the iffuing 2,000,000 of dollars to defray the expence of their military oppofition. Upon receiving an account that the people of North Carolina were very generally difaffected to their meafures, they directed a thoufand men to be raifed to fubdue the fpirit of oppofition in that Province; and they ordered the militia of the feveral Colonies to be embodied.

Having thus, with great fuccefs, brought their fcheme to a confiderable degree of maturity, all the difaffected to their meafures being difarmed, and a confiderable military force under their command in the field, they proceeded to make a formal declaration of war against their Sovereign and his Parliament, and to write another seditious letter to the people of Great Britain, to amuse or delude them into rebellion. These measures were of too much importance not to be communicated immediately to their faithful allies in Britain. A letter was therefore sent to the Lord Mayor, Aldermen, and Livery of London, paying them the " just tribute of " gratitude and thanks for the virtuous and " unsolicited resentment they had shewn to the " violated rights of a free people." And to convince the Corporation how sensible the Congress were " of the powerful aid their cause " must receive from such advocates," another letter was wrote to Mr. Penn, formerly Governor of Pennsylvania, who was then coming to England, and to the Colony agents, inclosing the declaration of war, the seditious letter to the people of Great-Britain, and that to the Lord Mayor. In this letter, the persons to whom it was directed were desired to put the declaration of war, and the letter to the people of Great-Britain, " immediately to the press, and " to communicate them as universally as possible." And they were also ordered to " give " such intelligence as they might judge to be " of importance to America in this great " contest*."

With this letter another petition was also sent to his Majesty, which, like those that had preceded it, was truly an insult and mockery. It was vague in respect to the subject matter, false in respect to a number of facts, indecisive as to American rights, and, though called a petition, asked for nothing. All these truths

* See Appendix.

will

will appear from a ſlight examination of the petition itſelf. It begins in theſe words: "We your "Majeſty's faithful ſubjects of the Colonies," &c. &c. Now can any man of ſenſe and candour be perſuaded that theſe men, notwithſtanding their profeſſions, could poſſibly be the "faithful ſubjects" of the King, when they denied their ſubordination to the Parliament, of which the King is head and ſupreme repreſentative? Could they, in the nature of things, be faithful to the repreſentative, while they withheld their obedience to the principal? Could they be faithful to the King, when they had taken up arms to oppoſe the authority of that ſupremacy in which he participates, and of which he is the ſupreme executive repreſentative? It is an abſurdity; a falſity too glaring to impoſe on a vulgar underſtanding.

In the next paragraph they wildly talk of an "union between the Mother Country and the "Colonies," and in another declare, that they are moſt "ardently deſirous that the former "harmony between them may be reſtored." But there is not the leaſt hint what kind of union they wiſhed for, or by what means that harmony might be reſtored. This they had avoided in all their petitions, becauſe they knew that Parliament was ready to meet any reaſonable propoſal of that nature. They could not mean a legiſlative union, or a ſubmiſſion to the ſame ſupreme authority, which is the only meaſure ever yet invented to combine the members of the ſame ſociety together; becauſe this they had uniformly denied. It muſt therefore be a fœderative union. Thus while they profeſſed themſelves felves subjects, they spoke in the language of allies, and were openly acting the part of enemies; and while in their petition they declared their subordination, by their actions they proved their design to be that of independence.

In their usual style of dissimulation they profess "too tender a regard for the kingdom from "which they derive their origin, to request "such a reconciliation as might be inconsistent "with her dignity or her welfare." What this reconciliation was, they have also avoided to mention. But so far as it is possible to collect it from their words and actions, we know it to be an exclusive right of legislation in their colonial assemblies. They had refused to be represented in the British Parliament; they had rejected a plan for establishing an American branch of that legislature, in which they would have been perfectly represented; they had rejected the proposition made by the House of Commons, leaving their colonial legislatures in the possession of the right of granting their contributions to the national defence in their own way. What other mode of reconciliation, consistent with the "dignity, or welfare of the kingdom," was now left? There was none which the powers of human reason could devise, short of independence.

Like their former petitions, this was not deficient in abuse of Administration. Their conduct was said to be replete with "delusive "pretences, fruitless terrors, and unavailing "severities;" that they had since the last war adopted "a *new system* of statutes and regula-"tions" to enslave the Colonies. But the

novelty

novelty of this ſyſtem they had not, in any of their proceedings, attempted to point out. The difference between the principles upon which the colonial adminiſtration has been managed ſince that period, from thoſe on which it had been managed before, remains yet a ſecret to all the world but the Congreſs. Indeed no aſſertion can be more groundleſs and falſe; becauſe every ſtatute and every colonial regulation ſince that time, is founded on a variety of precedents. Similar ſtatutes had been paſſed in former reigns, and ſome of them ſo early as the laſt century, and all of them had been cheerfully ſubmitted to by the Coloniſts, ſo that there was nothing novel in their principles. But this charge was neceſſary to deceive the people of both countries. It was neceſſary to raiſe ſome phantom of injuſtice, to prevail on Britons to give up rights which were as ancient as the ſettlement of America, and which the Americans by their conduct had always acknowledged; and it was neceſſary to induce the Americans to withdraw themſelves from that allegiance to Government, from whence they had derived their freedom, their ſafety and happineſs.

The prayer of the petition was vague, nugatory, and inſidious. They deſire his Majeſty "to point out ſome *mode*, by which the united "applications of his *faithful* Coloniſts to the "Throne may be improved into a happy and "permanent reconciliation." That men ſhould ſpeak of a reconciliation, who had never taken one ſtep towards it, and who had rejected the means of effecting it when offered, is remarkable. But what did they mean by *ſome mode?*

Was

Was it poſſible for his Majeſty, without the leaſt explanation, to divine what ideas they had annexed to theſe words? Did they mean the appointment of perſons to hear their complaints, and to redreſs them if juſt? They knew that the Parliament was the conſtitutional guardian of the rights of all the members of the empire, and poſſeſſed complete authority to redreſs their injuries, if any ſubſiſted; and therefore that it was their duty, as ſubjects, to define their rights, and to propoſe to the Parliament the means by which they deſired thoſe rights might be reſtored; and this very method had been pointed out to them by his Majeſty's Secretary of State, as we have ſeen in General Conway's letter. Did they mean that his Majeſty ſhould penetrate into their deſires, which they had artfully concealed? This was impoſſible. Did they mean that he ſhould make ſome propoſal, by which they might be enabled to grant their own aids, and be relieved from parliamentary taxation? This had been fully complied with, in the reſolution of the Houſe of Commons; and moreover, Commiſſioners who had eſpouſed their cauſe, and were friendly to their meaſures, were ſent over to confer on theſe and all other matters, and to make and receive propoſals. But even with theſe they refuſed to negociate in the character of ſubjects. They would not even confer but in their illegal, independent, and congreſſional capacity, inſidiouſly hoping to draw from the Commiſſioners a conceſſion of the legality and independence of their conſtitutions, the want of which had

hitherto

hitherto prevented the enemies of Britain from entering into an alliance with them.

Much clamour, ill-founded and unjuſt, has been made by the abettors of the American rebellion againſt his Majeſty's Miniſters, for not attending to this and other petitions equally nugatory, unmeaning, and affronting to the ſupreme authority of the State. I call this clamour ill-founded and unjuſt, becauſe the very faction who made it know, that in conſequence of the former petitions, the Houſe of Commons, diveſting itſelf of all reſentment at the indignity offered to the ſupreme authority of the State, by a denial of that authority, and a refuſal to participate in it, the greateſt it could poſſibly receive from its ſubjects, condeſcended to propoſe a plan which avoided theſe objections, was reaſonable and juſt, and would have been adopted as a ſufficient ground of negociation at leaſt, by men who were not reſolved on independence; and that, in purſuance of the laſt petition, Commiſſioners were ſent over with more enlarged powers, to negociate, and to know their as yet untold and latent deſires. And they alſo know, that the propoſition of the Houſe of Commons, made with the beſt intentions, and founded in the ſtricteſt juſtice, was loaded with the opprobrious terms "unreaſonable and inſidious;" and declared that it "was held up to the world to "deceive;" and that the ſubſequent commiſſion in the hands of their own friends was treated with equal inſult and neglect. The authors of this ill-founded abuſe upon Government, appear to have loſt all ſenſe of the practice and relative duties of ſubjects. If the American rights were infringed, it was most certainly their duty as subjects to define those rights, and to propose a remedy by which they might be restored. This was done by their fellow-subjects in Wales, Chester and Durham; it is done almost in every petition presented to Parliament for redress. Why then has it not been done by the American faction, if they were sincere in their professions, and desirous of an union with this country? Why has their whole conduct, from the beginning of the dispute, been dark, indecisive, hypocritical and insidious?

From this view of the facts it must appear evident, that there has been great, and indeed too much, condescension on the part of the State towards its subjects; that it has made advances towards a reconciliation as far as it possibly could, without giving up its essential rights, the rights of the people of Great-Britain, and discharging the Americans from all subordination; that from a lenity of disposition, and a desire to avoid the effusion of blood, they have overlooked, for a long time, insults greater in their nature than any which they would have received, without resentment, from any sovereign power whatever; while the Americans, relinquishing the characters of subjects, and laying aside all decency of language, have rested their pretensions on principles which, when candidly examined, clearly amount to a claim of absolute independence.

The Congress and their adherents, having dispatched the petition, proceeded in their military preparations with greater vigour, and more system. The Provincial Congresses, Conventions,

ventions, and Committees, became the executive authorities under them. These made daily advances in setting aside the established Governments, and in a short time assumed all their powers. Additions were made to their army. The republicans were embodied in arms, the loyalists were disarmed, and all the military stores and ammunition in America were collected in their magazines. Having taken his Majesty's fort at Ticonderoga, they invaded Canada, and besieged the British army in Boston.

Such was the general state of their affairs, when Congress received advice that British Commissioners were on their passage to America, empowered to offer to the Colonies terms of accommodation, and attended by a formidable military and naval force. They knew that a very great majority of the Colonists were attached to the British Government, and, though disarmed, would be ready to support the Commissioners as far as it was possible, in every reasonable proposal they should make. They saw the impossibility of obtaining their ultimate aim without foreign assistance, and that assistance they could not obtain even from the common and inveterate enemy of Britain, while they remained under the character of its subjects.

The necessity of their affairs now compelled them to throw off the mask. That design which they had disguised under the most solemn professions of loyalty, and of the most ardent desire to be united with Great-Britain on constitutional principles, ~~and which they had continually denied,~~ was now to be openly, and as ſolemnly avowed. To effect this in Congreſs, much cabal and intrigue was neceſſary. Many of the members, recollecting their inſtructions, knew the ſentiments of the people in general, and beſides ſaw the ruin and horrors of a meaſure ſo bold and dangerous. Their cabals continued near a month; the republican faction met with much oppoſition, and for a time, deſpaired of ſucceſs; at length, however, having made ſome proſelytes to their opinion, they reſolved to riſque the vote of Independence. And yet after all the arts of intrigue had been ſo long eſſayed, the queſtion was put, and the Colonies were equally divided. But upon the next day the queſtion being again reſumed, contrary to their own rules, Mr. Dickinſon, a gentleman naturally timid and variable in his principles, retracted his opinion, and gave the caſting vote. Thus did this great event, which was to ſupport a dangerous and ſeditious faction in the heart of the Mother Country, and to involve it in a war with two powerful nations, depend on the vote of an individual member of its own community.

The vote of Independence was ſoon followed by another, recommending to the people to aboliſh the old, and to inſtitute new forms of Government. This meaſure was eagerly adopted by their adherents, who had now all power in their own hands. They were combined in Congreſſes, Conventions, and Committees. They were arrayed in arms by voluntary aſſociations, and there was moreover a regular armed force under the Congreſs to ſupport them; while the loyaliſts, and friends to the Britiſh conſtitu-

tion,

tion, were without a head, and without weapons. These had been long since disarmed. The Governors of all the royal Colonies had been driven from their governments, while those of Pennsylvania, Rhode-Island, and Connecticut, were permitted to remain unmolested, and in office. The King's Governors had given opposition to their measures, while the others (excepting the Governor of Maryland) either had not disapproved of, or had openly abetted them. The Proprietary Governor of Pennsylvania, if he did not abet, did not, from the beginning of the sedition, discover the least disapprobation of their conduct. His friends, his magistrates, and all the officers of his own appointment, not ten in the whole Colony excepted, were leaders in the opposition. In the two Charter Governments of Rhode-Island and Connecticut, the Governors were the creatures of the faction, and at the head of their measures. All obstacles being thus removed, they were not long in establishing their new States, in which they excluded every trace of the powers of royalty and aristocracy.

The time was now come when the independent faction, having obtained by their arts sufficient power, were not afraid to acknowledge that they had deceived the people from the beginning of their opposition to Government; and that notwithstanding all their solemn professions to the contrary, they ever had independence in their view. Samuel Adams, the great director of their councils, and the most cautious, artful, and reserved man among them, did not hesitate, as soon as the vote of Independence had passed, to declare

declare in all companies, that “ he had laboured “ upwards of twenty years to accompliſh the “ meaſure; that during that time he had car- “ ried his art and induſtry ſo far, as to ſearch “ after every riſing genius in the New England “ ſeminaries, and employed his utmoſt abilities “ to fix in their minds the principles of Ame- “ rican Independence, and that he rejoiced he “ had now accompliſhed the meaſure.”

We have now before us a brief view of the principles of the American rebellion; and we find that it has riſen from the ſame ſource, and been conducted by the ſame ſpirit with that which effected the deſtruction of the Engliſh Government in the laſt century. The leaders in both ſet out with a pretence of aſſerting the liberties of the people. Profeſſions of the moſt zealous loyalty and firmeſt attachment to the eſtabliſhed Government, were the veils under which, for a time, they concealed their ſedition. The ſame arts and hypocritical falſehoods, with the ſame kind of illegal and tumultuous violence, were employed by both. Factious conventions, committees and mobs, were the inſtruments by which they carried their treaſonable practices into execution. If the pulpits of the ſectaries in England in the year 1641, reſounded with ſedition, the pulpits of the Congregational Independents and Preſbyterians, from Nova Scotia to Georgia, rung with the ſame flagitious doctrines. Upon a faithful enquiry it was found, that in the four New England Provinces, there were only twelve among five hundred and fifty diſſenting miniſters, and in all the other Colonies a ſtill leſs number, who declined

declined the rebellious task. If the opposition to the rebellion in England was composed chiefly of the members of the established Church, the same people, with the Quakers, Methodists, &c. as soon as their scheme of Independence was known, formed the opposition in America. And if the abolition of the monarchical and aristocratical parts of the constitution was the great object of the independents in Britain, all the circumstances attending the American rebellion added to the event, prove incontestibly, that the American republicans had the same design from the beginning constantly in their view.

The parallel between these rebellions might be carried yet further, but enough has been said to place the motives and designs of the American insurgents in their true light. If indeed there was any difference between them, it has consisted in the different conduct of the Princes, in whose reigns they have respectively happened, towards the insurgents. In the reign of Charles the First, it must be acknowledged that there were grievances which afforded a plausible pretext for opposition, though they could not justify the extent to which it was carried. Among these may be reckoned the frequent dissolutions of Parliament, the raising of money without the assent of Parliament; the proceedings against some of its members, and a variety of other transactions which did not consist with the freedom of the British constitution. But in the present reign there has been no one act which has had the least tendency, or which has discovered the least wish in the Prince or his Ministers to injure the constitution of the British Government, or to oppress the insurgents; but on the contrary, there have been the strongest proofs of a desire to preserve the constitution pure and inviolate. It has been a reign of the most ample protection, without one act of oppression or injustice.

Having thus traced the American rebellion from its original source to the declaration of Independence, I shall conclude these reflections with some general observations, which naturally arise out of the subject.

I know it is the opinion of some men, that Colonies cannot be long kept in subordination to the Parent State. That, like individuals in the different stages of life, they will in their youth be subordinate; but as soon as they are arrived at strength and maturity, they will naturally become discontented, and throw off their connexion with their Parent State. This opinion I have ever thought ill-founded. It is not supported by any instances to be found in ancient or modern history. The revolt of Colonies has ever been occasioned by other causes. The Colonies of Rome were oppressed; they were compelled to pay excessive tributes. These were levied by their Governors appointed at Rome. They furnished armies for the protection of the city, consisting of double the numbers supplied by Rome itself; and yet they did not participate in the rights of Roman citizens. They were neither enrolled in their legions, nor could vote in their Comitia; they were deprived of any possibility of sharing in the emoluments, honours, or dignities of office they were not even treated as members of the State,

State, but as ſlaves; and although they had often ſolicited the ſenate to give them the rights of citizens, the pride, the folly of the ſenate rejected their ſupplications, and therefore they revolted.

The great miſtake of Rome in the government of their Colonies and Provinces, was founded in the arrogance of power. Rome ſent out colonies, becauſe the principal territory was too full of inhabitants. She ſelected for this purpoſe the loweſt and the meaneſt of the people. Theſe, and thoſe whom her arms had lately conquered, her pride conſidered as an inferior claſs of mortals, not intitled to the rights of humanity. They were therefore indulged with few privileges. The State never conſidered that in time, by cultivating the ſame arts, and by their ſuperior induſtry, which the ſituation they were placed in tended to promote, they would become equally improved in knowledge, and poſſeſſed of equal, if not ſuperior power; and that when this ſhould happen, they would naturally perceive and reſent the illiberal and odious diſtinctions made between them and the other members of the State. To this folly the revolt of the Roman Colonies can only be juſtly attributed.

The revolt of the Britiſh Colonies has ariſen, as we have ſeen, from oppoſite cauſes. It is not uncommon for contrary extremes to produce the ſame effects. If the Romans gave leſs freedom to the coloniſt than the citizen enjoyed at Rome, Britons gave more liberty to the Americans than the ſubject enjoyed in Britain. Inſtead of giving them the ſame privileges, and ſubjecting them to the ſame powers to which the ſubjects in Britain were ſubordinate, they gave them rights which, if they did not amount to independence itſelf, approached as near as poſſible to it. Inſtead of enſlaving them, they gave them more freedom than was conſiſtent with true civil liberty.

Let us ſuppoſe that Rome or Britain had wiſely eſtabliſhed in their reſpective Colonies or Provinces, as ſoon as they were ſettled or conquered, ſyſtems ſimilar in eſſential polity to thoſe of the State, and had incorporated thoſe ſyſtems with the State itſelf; and that they had been governed by the ſame general laws and cuſtoms, and ſuffered to enjoy the ſame degree of liberty, excluding all diſtinctions between the citizen and the coloniſt; is there any perſon, acquainted with the influence and effects which civil polity ever had on the conduct of men, who can believe that either revolt would have happened? It does not conſiſt with reaſon, and ſtands contradicted by all experience.

The conduct of the Roman Colonies towards the State after their union with it, is a proof of this truth. For although their incorporation was rather partial than perfect; although inſtead of being united to the old, they were formed into a few new tribes, and were only admitted to vote laſt in order, ſo that they ſeldom had an opportunity of exerciſing their rights; yet ever after they ſupplied their proportions of men in the Roman armies, and their proportion of aids in the public treaſury; they fought her battles, and remained faithful to the State until they were ſevered from it by foreign violence, and the empire itſelf, enfeebled by the immenſe wealth and univerſal luxury and diſſipation of its people, was over-run by barbarous nations.

But we need not travel into ancient hiſtory to ſupport this truth. The inſtance of Scotland is within our memory. The extenſion of the Britiſh ſyſtem of government to that country we have ſeen continually operating on the manners and affections of the people; ſuppreſſing their former diſlike, and changing their averſion into a fixed affection for the State in ſo remarkable a manner, that from the moſt diſaffected of Britiſh ſubjects, they are become the moſt faithful, and in all probability will be the firmeſt friends to that conſtitution of which they have ſo lately been made partakers, when it ſhall ſtand in the moſt need of ſupport.

If theſe obſervations are juſt, there can be no reaſon to doubt but that the Colonies, ſhould they be reduced, may, by proper meaſures, be ſecured in their obedience to the Britiſh State for ages to come. The cauſes of the revolt being perfectly aſcertained, the political phyſician cannot be at a loſs for the proper remedy, nor deſpair of a cure. Upon looking into the ſtate of the patient, he will find every ſymptom in his favour. The poiſon has not ſpread itſelf through the general maſs of the people; the diſaffection is confined to two ſects of diſſenters; while the people of the Eſtabliſhed Churh, Methodiſts, Lutherans, German Calviniſts, Quakers, Menoniſts, &c. are warmly attached to the Britiſh Government, and ready to embrace any reaſonable terms which ſhall remove the conſtitutional defect in the authority of Parliament, the inability of the Colonies, and the causes of future revolt. In short, the Colonies at this moment are in that very disposition in which Charles II. found the people of Britain at the time of his restoration. They have seen the arts and frauds of their leaders, and are daily suffering under their treachery and tyranny; their country has been drained of its labourers, and remains uncultivated; their commerce is ruined, and every necessary of life is extravagantly dear, and but few to be obtained; and to increase this part of their distress, the little property remaining is daily seized, and nothing returned for it but money of no value, insomuch that they have wasted upwards of 40,000,000*l.* sterling in forging their own chains. Laws the most unjust, oppressive, and sanguinary, have been made for their government. Children have been driven from their parents, and husbands from their wives, into the field, to support the tyranny of their rulers; and more than one fifth part of their white inhabitants who were capable of bearing arms, have already perished in a war, unjust and unnatural. Disarmed, ruined, and incapable of assisting themselves, *they are looking up to Great Britain with impatience for deliverance from yet more grievous misfortunes.* In this situation, no man of reflection can doubt but that these unhappy people are ready to accept any just propositions for removing their distress, and giving them future safety; nor is it possible not to see, that this is the critical moment which Government ought to embrace for establishing that system of polity in the Colonies which will hereafter secure them to Great-Britain.

This disposition in the Americans, Government will certainly meet with propositions which shall give them reasonable liberty, and more firmly unite them to Great-Britain.

In order to effect these great purposes, temporary expedients, so often tried and so often ineffectual, must be avoided. These kinds of remedies are unworthy of wisdom; they have never yet failed to produce greater difficulties than they were intended to remove. The remedy should be such as to meet the disease, and to eradicate its causes. If it does not do this, it effects nothing, or something worse than nothing; it leaves the disorder to break out again at some future period, with redoubled virulence.

The inexpedience of the remedies hitherto applied will appear evident, if an individual may presume to canvass the resolutions of the State. The matters in dispute between the two countries lie in a very narrow compass. They may be all reduced to one great object, *viz. The right of the supreme authority of the State over the Colonies.* The statesman in Britain contends, and justly contends, *for the necessity of a supreme authority over every part and member of the empire.* In this he is supported by all precedents, by every known system of polity, by the reason and nature of civil society, and by the concurrent authority of all writers on Government. On the contrary, the Americans assert, that by the constitution of the English Government, settled and confirmed by the great Charter of Rights, it is essential to the freedom of America, that its landed interest or freeholders should be *represented* in the great

Councils,

Councils, which make the laws by which *their properties, their liberties, and their lives are to be affected*; and that without this the British Government is certainly *despotic* over them. Now these propositions are both true; and while the parties rest on them, it is impossible that an union, on principles of genuine policy, should ever take place. They are so repugnant, that they cannot be reconciled of themselves, without some intermediate proposition *which shall include the affirmative of both*—or which shall leave the parliamentary authority *supreme* over the Colonies, and at the same time give the Colonies a *representation*.

None of the measures proposed by Great-Britain to the Colonies have tended to these purposes. The proposition of the House of Commons in the year 1776, did neither give up the authority of Parliament, nor constitutionally modify it, but ultimately retained it on those very principles on which the Americans had denied it. The Colonies were left in the possession of the right which they had exercised before, of granting aids to the Crown; but if those aids were not approved by Parliament, its right to tax them, though not represented, remained in full force. Besides, this proposition related only to the right of taxing the Colonies, but the denial of the authority of Parliament regarded all legislative acts over them. Nor was the political incompetency of the Colonies, arising from their disunion, in any degree removed. Hence, however the proposition might and ought to have served as a ground for negociation,

ciation, it did not meet, nor tend to remove, the great object of dispute.

From one extreme Great-Britain, pushed on by a number of events as unexpected as unfortunate, ran into another. Dismayed at a series of ill successes in America, occasioned by the misconduct of her Generals, and the hostile declaration of France, and totally misinformed, by the arts of the factions on both sides of the Atlantic, in respect to the desires of the Americans in general, the terms next offered, so far as they were made known, if they did not amount to absolute independence, were little short of it. The right of Parliament to tax the Colonies was explicitly given up. The instructions of the Americans to their delegates in Congress, the repeated declarations of Congress before, and even at the time of their declaring their independence, to be more firmly united *on constitutional principles*, were forgot, and all that Government seemed to expect was a fœderative "*union of force*" between the two countries. If Great-Britain was too tenacious of the ancient authority of Parliament in the first, she was too inattentive to her rights in the last propositions. If she fell short of the wishes of the Colonists in general in the first, she infinitely surpassed them in the last; so that none of them were agreeable to the people in general of America, because they did not contain any ground upon which might be erected a *constitutional union* between the two countries. They did not meet the allegations of the parties, nor tend in any degree to reconcile the difference.

These

These propositions were not only defective, but ill-timed. If the British councils had shewn a determined firmness to maintain the authority of Parliament in the time of the Stamp Act, and had then offered the resolution of the House of Commons, it would in all probability have been made the ground of negociation. The republican faction was not then formed, or prepared for military opposition, and must therefore have submitted or treated. And had the propositions sent over by the last Commissioners been made before the independents had received assurances of assistance from France, they would certainly have been accepted by them; but at the time they were made, the Congress had formed their alliance with France. They had seen the unparalleled blunders of the British commander, the evacuation of Philadelphia, and the retreat of the British army to New-York; and upon being informed of the purport of the terms then offered, they perceived that Parliament had given up its authority; that the councils of the British State were yielding to their wishes; and they were confirmed in this opinion by letters wrote by the faction in Britain, *assuring them that if they persevered, they must in the end obtain absolute independence.*

It was not probable that propositions, both defective and ill-timed, would meet with the concurrence of the persons to whom they were made. The Americans were now divided in two parties. The first, and by far the greatest, consisted of men who had severely felt the tyranny and cruelties of their new rulers, and sincerely wished for an union with Great-Britain on the fundamental

fundamental and essential principles of the English Government. The second were men whom nothing less than perfect independence would satisfy. The loyalists did not wish that the authority of Parliament, in any respect, should be absolutely given up. All that they desired was, that it might be modified, and made more constitutional over them." An union, and not a separation in polity, was the object of their pursuit. But the terms offered did not contain any principles on which the two countries could be united; on the contrary, they, to all appearance, laid a sure foundation of future quarrel and civil wars, and consequently of American independence; an event equally inconsistent with their safety and happiness as with that of Great Britain. They therefore preferred the temporary ravages and horrors of war to the lasting mischiefs which these propositions, if accepted, must have entailed on them and their posterity.

On the other hand, the independents now grown desperate from their rebellion, and the innumerable cruelties committed on the loyalists, equally reprobated them, because they hoped, by the assistance of France, soon to obtain the great object of their original design, and to support their own power and dignity, which they knew they must resign if a reconciliation with Great Britain should take place. Hence it happened, that there never were any proposals of accommodation held out by one people to another, more universally disapproved than the terms of the last commission.

Seeing then that those temporary and defective expedients have failed in settling the difference between the two countries, Great-Britain will certainly purſue other meaſures more promiſing of ſucceſs. A little conſideration will tell her, that it is not a confederation of force, or a commercial alliance, but a firm and ſolid union in polity, which only can ſecure the Colonies. And in order to know upon what principles this union ought to be eſtabliſhed, we are not to ſearch for them in the laws of nature and nations; they are to be found nearer home. Thoſe principles upon which all civil ſocieties are formed, and particularly thoſe upon which the Britiſh conſtitution is eſtabliſhed, will beſt inſtruct us. Here we ſhall find,

That a *ſupreme legiſlative authority* over every member and part of a ſociety, in reſpect to every matter ſuſceptible of human direction, is eſſential in the conſtitution of all States. That it is this authority, the ſame fundamental principles of polity, and the ſame general laws pervading the whole ſyſtem, whatever may be its form, which create in the ſubjects the ſame habits, manners, affections and prejudices, fix the national attachment, form the cement of union, and by an imperceptible impulſe compel them to act, on all occaſions, in concert for the common good and ſafety: And that to give up one of the rights of this authority, and more eſpecially the moſt important of all, the right of taxation, will be only the prelude to a ſpeedy ſurrender of the whole.

We ſhall here alſo perceive, that the Britiſh Government is a mixed monarchy, in which the principles of the three ſimple forms of Government are ſo wiſely mixed and tempered, as to

guard.

guard, with equal power and certainty, againſt the two great enemies to civil liberty, deſpotiſm and licentiouſneſs. That a repreſentation in its ſupreme authority is the eſſence of its freedom; and that its power over a diſtrict of territory whoſe people are not repreſented, is deſpotic, and not free.

Upon conſidering the nature and deſign of inferior and ſubordinate ſocieties, we ſhall find, that they are intended to ſupport and ſtrengthen the principal ſyſtem, and not to weaken, oppoſe, or to deſtroy it; and therefore that they ſhould be formed on the principles and fundamental laws of the State itſelf. That inferior democratical ſocieties, or thoſe whoſe powers and rights are not properly mixed and balanced, cannot ſtrengthen, but muſt weaken a mixed form of Government. That the ſimple principles of ariſtocracy or democracy will not ſuit under a monarchy, and ſo *mutatis mutandis*; nor will the principles of any of them unmixed, and not duly balanced, agree with a mixed monarchy,

Upon looking into the Governments of the Colonies before they were annulled by the rebellion, we ſhall perceive that they were a chaos of political abſurdities, conſonant to no ſyſtems ever yet invented; that they neither harmonized with each other, nor with the State itſelf; and that they have been ſettled through the indolence, or ignorance, or corruption of former politicians, on principles totally heterogeneous and repugnant to thoſe of the Government to which they were intended to be ſubordinate. In the Royal Colonies, the powers of Government are divided between the repreſentative of the Crown and the people, without the leaſt intermediate check to an exceſs of conſtitutional power in either. In the Proprietary Colonies, the regal power, or the repreſentative of the Britiſh State, has ſcarcely retained the ſhadow of its authority. All the executive and fœderative rights of the State are granted to the proprietaries and *their heirs*, and all the powers of complete legiſlation are divided between them and the people, without any mean check or controul. In one of the Charter Colonies, the repreſentative of the Britiſh State has very little more weight in the legiſlative and executive powers, than the Doge has in the councils of *Venice*; and in the other two the Governments are, to all intents and purpoſes, independent democracies; ſo that they are truly ſo many *inferior political monſters, which have, and ever will coaleſce to diſturb the peace and order of the ſociety, and in the end to deſtroy it.*

And we muſt further conſider, that men can only be governed either by fear or art. That fear muſt be ſupported by force, and that force will not anſwer our preſent purpoſe. For, however it may be uſed with ſucceſs by deſpotic Governments, it cannot be ſafely employed in one where freedom conſtitutes its eſſence, and a great number of people are to be governed by it. We muſt therefore apply to policy for the means by which the two countries muſt be united, if united for any ſeries of time. This will teach us to remove, as much as poſſible, all diſtinctions in reſpect to the power, rights and privileges, which have too long ſubſiſted between a ſuba ſubject in Britain and one in America, and conſequently to carry over the Atlantic the ſame fundamental rights and powers, the ſame conſtitutional privileges, the ſame general laws and maxims of polity, under and by which the habits and manners, the paſſions and attachments of the ſubject in Britain have been formed, directed and governed; becauſe it is this policy alone that can eradicate that averſion to a mixed monarchy which has been ſuffered to exiſt already too long in the Colonies, and which can form a ſolid and permanent union between the two countries, *making them one people of one mind, in reſpect to their common intereſt and ſafety.*

It is much to be regretted, that neither country ſeems to approve of an American repreſentation in Parliament, becauſe it is a meaſure the moſt conſiſtent with thoſe principles upon which the unity and freedom of the Britiſh Government is eſtabliſhed. However, ſince this is deſpaired of, it will be wiſdom, ſecondary wiſdom at leaſt, to adopt the next beſt. An American legiſlature, incorporated with the Britiſh Parliament, for the purpoſes of American regulations, in which the Coloniſts ſhall be repreſented, and in which they ſhall be capable of giving validity to no act but what ſhall be approved of by Parliament, is that meaſure. Indeed there is no other ſolid, or even rational mode of union in polity, except a repreſentation in Parliament. It is this joint conſent which conſtitutes the unity of the Britiſh, and of every other mixed form of Government.

By

By this legiſlature, if properly conſtituted, the rights which the Americans claim may be reſtored, their political inability to grant their reaſonable proportions of aids towards the national defence may be removed, a ſecurity that they will give thoſe aids on all occaſions may be obtained; and their ſubordination to the Britiſh State may be eſtabliſhed on ſuch principles as will unite them with Great-Britain for ages to come.

Sincerely diſpoſed, as the greater part of the people in America are, to be more firmly united with Great-Britain on conſtitutional principles, is it not much to be lamented, that the Britiſh legiſlature, ſeeing the defect in its conſtitutional authority over the Colonies, and knowing that it is the great foundation of their diſcontent, have not taken it into their ſerious conſideration, and adopted the meaſure moſt proper for removing it? Had this been done in the beginning of the oppoſition to the authority of Parliament, the republican faction muſt have been deſtitute of the means by which they have inflamed the minds of the Americans, and led them to a revolt. But I am not fond of dwelling on paſt errors, further than is neceſſary to amendment. It is not now too late; and perhaps, all circumſtances conſidered, this is the moſt proper time for doing it. The ſtrong deſires of the people, the ſeverity of their new laws, the ſuperlative tyranny of their rulers, the extreme diſtreſs they have ſuffered, and are likely to ſuffer, and the apprehenſions they juſtly entertain of the inſidious deſigns of the courts of Verſailles and Madrid, point out this as the fortunate moment. Men tired of their present misery, and having yet greater in proſpect, will cheerfully embrace ſuch propoſals as evidently tend to their future ſafety and happineſs. Beſides, a meaſure of this kind will falſify the declaration of Congreſs conſtantly held up to the people, that the Parliament intends to enſlave them. It cannot fail to remove their fears, and fix a confidence in the juſtice and upright intentions of the State towards them; and it muſt do more *towards breaking the confederacy of the Colonies*, and reſtoring their obedience to Government, than any other meaſure that can be poſſibly deviſed.

The remarkable ſucceſs of this policy, when adopted by Rome on a ſimilar occaſion, will, I truſt, prove a leſſon of inſtruction to Britain. The ſupreme authority of that city was abſolute over her Colonies and Provinces. A conſtitutional participation in the rights of that authority, though poſſeſſed by the citizens, was imprudently withheld from the coloniſts. This diſtinction, in reſpect to their politic rights, gave great diſcontent to the latter. To obtain the ſame rights which were enjoyed by their fellow-ſubjects in Rome, they entered into a confederacy, and took arms. The *Social war* enſued. Many battles were fought; the coloniſts often triumphed; and Rome was reduced to the greateſt extremity. At length her obſtinacy and folly gave way to her ſafety. A law was paſſed, called the *Lex Julia*, becauſe propoſed and obtained by Lucius Julius Cæſar, granting to ſuch of the Colonies as ſhould lay down their arms, the *conſtitutional rights of Ro-*

man citizens. This law being immediately communicated to the Colonies, what were the consequences? Those Colonies which were tired of the war, those which were content with the terms offered, and those which wished to be united with Rome, although the mode of the grant was not perfectly agreeable to them, laid down their arms, deserted the union, and returned to their former obedience. And Rome, whose armies had been defeated in almost every battle, now, and not till now, triumphed in her turn; and soon after, honourably to herself, ended the war, and recovered her lost authority over her Colonies. All this she performed, although, like Britain, civil broils and factions engaged her councils at home, and a dangerous combination of two powerful Princes, the Kings of Pontus and Armenia, employed her arms abroad.

This policy, this act of public justice to her subjects, together with a firmness of spirit which "*never despaired of the commonwealth,*" saved Rome, and in all probability, if pursued, will save Britain. The same causes will ever produce the same effects. Should Great-Britain offer to the Americans a civil constitution, containing a measure of power, and a degree of liberty commensurate to her own polity, excluding all distinctions between Britons and Americans, and removing the great cause of colonial complaints, is there not the strongest of all probabilities, to induce us to believe, that it will produce the same happy effects which the like measure produced in the Roman Colonies? If this measure,

proposed

proposed to a people, at a time when their arms were crowned with victories, and when the State which they were opposing was reduced to the greatest difficulties, could recal to their minds their former connections; could remove their fears excited by frequent denials of their reasonable petitions; could revive their former attachments and affections; could dissever their union, and bring them home to their obedience; surely there is more reason to convince us that the Americans, dreading the ambitious designs of their insidious ally; destitute of the great resources of war; without men, and without money; their commerce lost, their forces generally defeated, and their country ruined by the ravages and expences of the war, will see their own interest, and embrace those terms when offered which they would have accepted in the time of their prosperity.

Should it be objected, that the most liberal terms of accommodation have been already offered without effect, my answer is, that proposals for accommodating a dispute of such magnitude and importance to both countries, should not only be properly timed, but explicit, and clear from all ambiguity. They should also fully and equitably meet the subject matter in controversy, and, if possible, the wishes of the people to whom they are made. Now none of the terms offered to the Americans came within these descriptions, as I have before shewn. If then we have been guilty of mistakes through the want of right information, we certainly ought not to suffer those mistakes to prevent our taking such measures as we ought to have taken at firſt. Rome at length found it neceſſary to her ſafety to be juſt, and to do that in her diſtreſs, with little credit to herſelf, which ſhe might and ought to have done in her proſperity, with greater advantage and better grace. Had Rome continued obſtinate, or had ſhe ultimately offered to her Colonies equivocal and inadequate propoſitions, her glory, if not her exiſtence, muſt have been ſacrificed to her obſtinacy and folly.

Why then ſhould not Great-Britain, when involved in the ſame difficulties, attended by the ſame circumſtances, and having the ſame proſpect of ſucceſs before her, follow a precedent which promiſes ſuch beneficial conſequences? Is it becauſe the earneſt wiſh of the people of America is not known? This cannot be the caſe, becauſe it is fully aſſerted in their inſtructions to their delegates in Congreſs, and a variety of other public documents, and declared to be a *conſtitutional union in polity with Great-Britain.* Is it becauſe the Congreſs have artfully avoided to gratify the deſires of the people in explicitly aſking for that union, or becauſe they have inſolently refuſed to treat with this country, contrary to the general ſenſe of their conſtituents? Both theſe reaſons are the ſtrongeſt that can be offered in favour of the meaſure. Is it becauſe a meaſure, which evidently tends to break the confederated force and union of the colonies—to remove the fears of the loyaliſts, and to gratify their reaſonable deſires, which perfectly coincide with the true intereſt and permanent ſafety of both countries, is unworthy of the ſerious deliberations of a

British

Britiſh Parliament? Or is it becauſe a ſeditious faction within the bowels of the State, by their intrigues and cabals, ſo inceſſantly engroſſes the time, and diſtracts the councils of Parliament, that it cannot purſue thoſe means which the dictates of reaſon and common ſenſe point out as neceſſary to the ſafety of the empire?

Whatever may have been the reaſons that no adequate propoſitions, no terms which could lead to a more conſtitutional union between the two countries, have been ſettled in the Britiſh councils, and tendered to the Americans, it is certainly high time, after a four years military conteſt, that it ſhould be done. True wiſdom directs, that reformation ſhould take place as ſoon as defects and miſtakes are known. A procraſtination of remedy ever gives to the evil intended to be removed, time to encreaſe, and often places it beyond the reach of the moſt perfect ſkill.

To conclude theſe reflections: When I take a view of the preſent ſtate of Europe, nothing is wanting to convince me, that the welfare and exiſtence of Great-Britain as an independent empire, depend on the recovery of her loſt authority over the Colonies, and on a more perfect union with them.

When I conſider the principles which ever did, and ever muſt bind the ſeveral parts of civil ſociety together, I am alſo convinced, that the duration of that union muſt depend on the principles of polity by which the two countries ſhall be united, and that it will be longer or ſhorter as thoſe principles accord or diſagree with the fundamental rights upon which the British Government is established.

And when I reflect on the present state of the Colonies, I am equally satisfied that this is the favourable moment for settling that union, and securing the subordination of the Colonies to the latest period of the British Government.

Impressed with these sentiments, I have been induced to lay the foregoing facts and reflections before the Public. I have briefly recited the causes of the present rebellion—the means by which it has grown to its present maturity—the state of American parties—the disposition of the Colonists; to which I have added some general remarks on the incompetency of the measures proposed for reconciling the unfortunate dispute between the two countries, and on the prospect of success which other measures, founded in the merits of the dispute, must be attended with. If, in doing this, I shall have contributed to throw any light on the subject, or to point out those measures which will unite the two countries together, my purpose will be attained.

APPENDIX.

APPENDIX.

EXTRACTS from the JOURNALS of the AMERICAN CONGRESS.

Saturday, July the 8th, 1775.

THE letter to the Lord Mayor, Aldermen, and Livery of London, being again read and debated, was agreed to as follows:

"My Lord,

"Permit the delegates of the people of Twelve ancient Colonies to pay your Lordſhip, and the very reſpectable body of which you are the head, *the juſt tribute of gratitude and thanks for the virtuous and unſolicited reſentment you have ſhewn to the violated rights of a free people.* The city of London, my Lord, having in all ages approved itſelf the patron of liberty, and the ſupport of juſt government againſt lawleſs tyranny and oppreſſion, *cannot fail to make us deeply ſenſible of the powerful aid our cauſe muſt receive from ſuch advocates.* A cauſe, my Lord, worthy of the ſupport of the firſt city in the world, as it involves the fate of a great continent, and *threatens to ſhake the foundations of a flouriſhing, and until lately a happy empire.*

"North

"North America, my Lord, wishes most ardently for a lasting connection with Great-Britain on terms of just and equal liberty; less than which generous minds will not offer, nor brave and free ones be willing to receive.

"A cruel war has at length been opened against us; and whilst we prepare to defend ourselves like the descendants of Britons, we still hope that the mediation of wise and good citizens will at length prevail over despotism, and restore harmony and peace on permanent principles to an oppressed and divided empire.

We have the honour to be,
My Lord, with great esteem,
Your Lordship's *faithful friends*
And *fellow subjects.*"

Ordered--That the above be transcribed; and then signed by the President.

The committee appointed to prepare a letter to Mr. Penn, and the colony agents, reported a draught, which was read and approved, as follows:

"Gentlemen,

"The perseverance of the British Ministry in their unjust and cruel system of Colony administration, has occasioned the meeting of another Congress.

"We have again appealed to the justice of our Sovereign for protection against the destruction which his Ministers meditate for his American subjects. This petition you will please, Gentlemen, to present to the King with all convenient expedition, *after which we desire*

it

it may be given to the Public. We likewiſe ſend you our ſecond application to the *equity and intereſt* of our fellow-ſubjects in Great-Britain, and alſo a DECLARATION *ſetting forth the cauſes of our taking up arms*; both which we wiſh may be *immediately put to the preſs, and communicated* AS UNIVERSALLY AS POSSIBLE.

" The Congreſs entertain the *higheſt ſenſe* of the WISE and WORTHY *interpoſition of the Lord Mayor and Livery of London in favour of* INJURED AMERICA. They have expreſſed this *their ſenſe*, in a letter to his Lordſhip and the Livery, *which we deſire may be preſented in a manner moſt agreeable to that* RESPECTABLE BODY.

" You will oblige us, Gentlemen, by giving the moſt *early information to the Congreſs, and to the Speakers of our reſpective aſſemblies, of your proceeding in this buſineſs*; and *ſuch further intelligence as you may judge to be of importance to America in this GREAT conteſt.*

We are, with great regard,

Gentlemen, &c."

Ordered—That the above be fairly tranſcribed, and then ſigned by the Preſident, and by him ſent under cover, together with the *Petition to the King*, and *Addreſs to the Inhabitants of Great-Britain*, and the Letter to the *Lord Mayor*, &c. to Richard Penn, Eſq; and that the Preſident requeſt Mr. Penn, in *behalf of the Congreſs*, to join with the Colony agents in preſenting the Petition to the King.

F I N I S.

www.ingramcontent.com/pod-product-compliance
Lightning Source LLC
Chambersburg PA
CBHW030604270326
41927CB00007B/1039